What people are saying about …

It's No Secret

"I used Rachel Olsen's *It's No Secret* for my personal quiet time. The chapters and Bible study portions are a perfect fit for daily time with God. Rachel combines engaging stories with challenging thoughts for every woman."

Marybeth Whalen, director of SheReads for Proverbs 31 Ministries and author of *The Mailbox*

"With the heart of a teacher and the honesty and warmth of a girlfriend, Rachel unpacks the principles of faith and gives practical direction in applying these truths to everyday living."

Carol Davis, radio host on 106.9 The Light, a ministry of the Billy Graham Evangelistic Association

"This book might have been called *Real Life with Rachel* because it's like sitting down with your BFF as she leads you down paths you should have visited long ago and reminds you it is never too late to start again. Real life. Real friendship. Real Jesus revealed. I simply loved it!"

Shari Braendel, popular speaker at the What to Wear Christian women's conferences and Modest is Hottest fashion shows and author of *Good Girls Don't Have to Dress Bad*

"With engaging stories, an insightful perspective, and sound biblical teaching, Rachel Olsen's *It's No Secret* reveals the secrets of Christ's truth and, more importantly, Christ's heart. This is a book that I will return to when I want to be reminded of what matters most when living for God. This would be a great guide for personal quiet times or small groups."

Melanie Chitwood, speaker and writer
for Proverbs 31 Ministries and author of
What a Husband Needs from His Wife and
What a Wife Needs from Her Husband

"If you long to live an authentic life filled with purpose, marked by mission, and properly prioritized, *It's No Secret* will show you how. Rachel Olsen has created the ultimate godly girlfriends' guide—completely contemporary yet biblically solid; poignant yet practical. Her clever, warm, and vulnerable style imparts a fresh and needed dose of perspective to all of God's girls. My new favorite how-to-do-life-and-do-it-well book!"

Karen Ehman, national speaker for Proverbs
31 Ministries and Hearts at Home conferences
and author of *A Life That Says Welcome* and
*The Complete Guide to Getting and Staying
Organized,* www.KarenEhman.com

"Just a few chapters into *It's No Secret*, I felt like I was sitting with a wise and witty girlfriend who had opened her heart and drawn me in with memorable stories told in a spunky yet sensitive style. It's clear that Rachel Olsen cares about her readers and longs to share the secrets she's come to know—secrets that turn our eyes from worthless things to treasures of wisdom and knowledge. Pull up a chair and lean in close—whether Rachel is revealing truths about complexions, cakes, or community, you won't want to miss a word!"

Ann Kroeker, author of *Not So Fast: Slow-Down Solutions for Frenzied Families*

It's No Secret

It's No Secret

REVEALING DIVINE TRUTHS
EVERY WOMAN SHOULD KNOW

Rachel Olsen

David C Cook®

transforming lives together

IT'S NO SECRET
Published by David C. Cook
4050 Lee Vance View
Colorado Springs, CO 80918 U.S.A.

David C. Cook Distribution Canada
55 Woodslee Avenue, Paris, Ontario, Canada N3L 3E5

David C. Cook U.K., Kingsway Communications
Eastbourne, East Sussex BN23 6NT, England

David C. Cook and the graphic circle C logo
are registered trademarks of Cook Communications Ministries.

The Web site addresses recommended throughout this book are offered as a
resource to you. These Web sites are not intended in any way to be or imply an
endorsement on the part of David C. Cook, nor do we vouch for their content.

Unless otherwise indicated, all Scripture quotations are taken from the New Living
Translation of the Holy Bible. New Living Translation copyright © 1996 by Tyndale
Charitable Trust. Used by permission of Tyndale House Publishers. Scriptures
marked as CEV are taken from the *Contemporary English Version* © 1995 by American
Bible Society. Used by permission. Scripture quotations marked ESV are taken from
The Holy Bible, English Standard Version. Copyright © 2000; 2001 by Crossway
Bibles, a division of Good News Publishers. Used by permission. All rights reserved.
Scripture quotations marked MSG are taken from *THE MESSAGE*. Copyright © by
Eugene H. Peterson 1993, 1994, 1995, 1996, 2000, 2001, 2002. Used by permission
of NavPress Publishing Group. Scripture quotations marked NASB are taken from
the *New American Standard Bible*, © Copyright 1960, 1995 by The Lockman
Foundation. Used by permission. Scripture quotations marked NCV are taken from
the New Century Version. Copyright © 1987, 1988, 1991 by Word Publishing, a
division of Thomas Nelson, Inc. Used by permission. All rights reserved. Scripture
quotations marked NIV are taken from the *Holy Bible, New International Version*®.
NIV®. Copyright © 1973, 1978, 1984 International Bible Society. Used by
permission of Zondervan. All rights reserved. Scripture quotations marked NKJV are
taken from the New King James Version. Copyright © 1982 by Thomas Nelson, Inc.
Used by permission. All rights reserved. The author has added italics for emphasis.

LCCN 2010930103
ISBN 978-1-4347-6537-6
eISBN 978-1-4347-0259-3

Published in association with William K. Jensen Literary
Agency, 119 Bampton Court, Eugene, OR 97404.

The Team: Susan Tjaden, Amy Kiechlin, Sarah Schultz, Caitlyn York, Karen Athen
Cover Design: Nicole Weaver, Zeal Design Studio

Printed in the United States of America
First Edition 2010

2 3 4 5 6 7 8 9 10

050611

For my daughter, Alaina

My love for you fuels my pursuit of these "secrets" to godly womanhood.
Don't reject them just because Mom wrote them.

Contents

Acknowledgments

Thank you to my "Yahweh Sisterhood" at Proverbs 31 Ministries with whom I have explored, tested, and celebrated the secrets that follow. Doing life and ministry with you gals is one of my greatest blessings.

Deepest thanks to my P31 sister Samantha. Your passion for Scripture, good writing, and this project were exactly what I needed to see me through the completion of this book. I wouldn't have wanted to do this without you. I so appreciate you!

Special thanks also to Leslie for helping make me a better writer—and making that process a spa-like experience. And to Bill for making this project happen.

Warm thanks to my husband, Rick, for supporting me and helping to shape me into the woman I've become. To Alaina and Caleb, you two are my joy. To Jimmy Dick, I can't begin to thank you enough, for everything. And to Barbara, Briana, Kelly, and Whitney for making me want to sing "We Are Family" while dancing around like Sister Sledge.

Susan, Terry, and the team at David C. Cook, thank you for believing in my writing and message. I'm thrilled to partner with you in the quest for fostering life change through the power of the Word.

I want them to have full confidence
because they have complete understanding
of God's secret plan, which is Christ himself.
In him lie hidden all the treasures
of wisdom and knowledge. (Col. 2:2–3)

Introduction

Can I Tell You a Secret?

Psst … lean in a little closer, and make sure no one sees what you're reading. I'm going to tell you a secret: The sparkly 1.5-carat rock on my left ring finger is not a real diamond at all; it's made of moissanite.

But I like to pretend it's real.

You can't tell by looking at it that the stone is not a high-quality diamond. In fact, if you place moissanite under an electronic diamond tester, it will register as a diamond. Only someone specifically trained can tell the two stones apart. So my engagement ring has been my little secret, until now.

I've always wondered what people would think if they knew the truth about my ring. I have at least one friend who won't mind. While riding in the car with her for the first time, I couldn't help but notice her big diamond earrings. I told her they were stunning.

She tossed her head and laughed. "Honey, they're fake. In my book, jewelry doesn't have to have real gems; it just has to be real big and real sparkly."

"Amen!" I responded with the sincerest of convictions and a knowing nod. At that moment I knew we'd be great friends.

What is it about sharing a secret that bonds two people together? There's something thrilling about being trusted with personal information. It's a backstage pass to peer behind a friend's public facade into her heart. When a girlfriend tells me a secret, it weaves an intimate connection between us—a connection that requires me to be trustworthy and faithful in return. It reveals her true feelings about me. I feel chosen, honored, trusted, and even somewhat empowered by her revelation.

But did you ever stop to think that God stands ready to reveal many of His secrets to you? As He does He chooses you, honors you, trusts you, and empowers you.

Are you ready for a more intimate connection with Him? Can you respond with trust and faithfulness? Are you ready for some divine secrets?

God-Sized Secrets

A few days ago, a postcard came in the mail informing me of a "secret sale" at one of my favorite stores. It let me know that as a valuable customer, I'm permitted to shop the sale a day early. Needing a jacket to wear to an upcoming event, I made time to head to the shop and see what might be "in store" for me. All of their items are timeless, quality pieces, no passing fads in sight. What a dream it would be to have an abundance of their beautiful things!

Now imagine you've just received a postcard in the mail announcing a secret sale on God's knowledge. How would you feel? What would you do? Would you make time to gain an abundance of it? The twelve disciples received a similar announcement from Jesus, inviting them to gain deeper understanding of timeless truths.

As the disciples followed Jesus over time, listening to His teachings, they noticed a new pattern emerging in His speaking style. Initially He taught in a fairly straightforward manner. Later He began using stories to answer questions or to make important points. Quite often the stories He told confused the crowd and occasionally even the disciples. Could it be God's Son wasn't a gifted communicator? Was He just hit or miss with His teaching ability? Surely not. The disciples couldn't figure out His change in tactics.

They came to Him eager to know the reason. In Matthew 13:10 the disciples asked Jesus, "Why do you always tell stories when you talk to the people?" That's when Jesus dropped them a postcard, so to speak. He extends the same invitation to you and me:

> "You have been permitted to understand the secrets of the Kingdom of Heaven, but others have not. To those who are open to my teaching, more understanding will be given, and they will have an abundance of knowledge. But to those who are not listening, even what they have will be taken away from them. That is why I tell these stories, because people see what I do, but they don't really see. They hear what I say, but they don't really hear, and they don't understand." (vv. 11–13)

I have to admit at times I've felt like one of those people who prompted Jesus to teach in this manner. I'd listen to what the pastor said on a given Sunday but forget about it days or weeks later, never integrating it into my life. Occasionally, a passionate Bible teacher or a troubling circumstance would motivate me to read the Bible on my own, but often I felt I got nothing out of it. I'd read a few paragraphs, look up, and wonder what I was supposed to be learning. I'd close my Bible and go on with life until the next time someone or something motivated me to try again.

I've always been a good student, so why couldn't I understand more of the Bible? Did God give out secret decoder rings? Had I somehow failed to get one?

After reading Jesus' postcard announcement in Matthew 13, I realized there *is* some sort of a decoder ring. *But what is it?* I wondered. *How could I get it?* (And could mine be really sparkly?)

Jesus said there are secrets in the kingdom of God, and if we are open to His teaching, He'll help us understand them. The word *secrets* used here is translated from the Greek *musterion,* which means a sacred hidden truth that is naturally unknown to human reason but is made known by revelation of God. Therefore, it's not up to you or me to figure out the mysteries of God or the deep truths of the Bible with our own understanding. *Jesus* is our secret decoder ring!

Yahweh, as God is called in the Old Testament, never hides truth from sincere seekers. In fact, He came to earth in the person of Jesus to ensure that we'd learn His secrets and understand His ways. "For God, who said, 'Let there be light in the darkness,' has made us understand that this light is the brightness of the glory of God that is seen in the face of Jesus Christ'" (2 Cor. 4:6). Our task is to open ourselves—ears, eyes, and heart—and listen to Him. I don't know about you, but I have a hard time resisting secrets, especially God-sized secrets!

Opening Ears, Eyes, and Heart

One thing I enjoy about close friends is how we develop our own way of communicating. Certain words or phrases take on special meaning for us, like a girlfriends' code. What makes perfect sense to the two of us floats right over the heads of others nearby. Likewise, befriending Jesus—drawing close to Him over time—develops our ability to recognize His still, small voice. Our heart grows familiar with and closer to His, enabling us to understand His meaning when that used to float right over our heads.

The Bible assures us that no matter where we go in life, we are never out of earshot of Jesus' voice. If we've gotten to know Him, we'll always recognize it—as we would a long-lost friend on the other end of a telephone line. Not only will we recognize Jesus' voice—it will direct us: "Whether you turn to the right or to the left, your ears will hear a voice behind you, saying, 'This is the way; walk in it'" (Isa. 30:21).

God commanded Peter, James, and John (as well as you and me) to listen to Jesus. Yahweh knows that Jesus embodies everything we need to know. We can hear Him. Jesus Himself said, "My sheep listen to my voice; I know them, and they follow me" (John 10:27 NIV). Listening to Jesus is the only way we'll know how to live our lives as Yahweh's women, how to follow Him where He leads. In my experience, opening our ears fully to listen to Jesus takes us on grand adventures we scarcely could imagine.

Ageless Secrets

The secrets contained in the pages of this book are nothing new or hidden at all. They've all been wrapped within the Word of God and the person of Christ for thousands of years, readily accessible through the ages.

As the perceptive writer of Ecclesiastes said, "Nothing under the sun is truly new" (Eccl. 1:9). However, each new generation of women needs to encounter God and discover His truths for themselves. You and I must apply His teachings in the days we've been given under the sun. This is our quest. As we do, we uncover the glory of Yahweh, as well as our truest selves, and walk together into the kingdom of God.

In the pages of this book, you and I will find a dozen hidden treasures of wisdom Christ longs to reveal to us. These teachings run counter to what our culture tells us about successful living. I hope we will grasp each of these simple-yet-divine secrets for successful living in the kingdom of God, apply them, and share them with others.

These God-sized secrets contain the keys we are looking for— answers to the issues of modern life, such as exhausting schedules, unpaid bills, relational conflicts, and unmet expectations. These secrets, and their Source, are the solution to the longings of our souls.

Just as I've shared with you the secret about my diamond ring, God eagerly waits to share with us great secrets from His Word. Before we continue, however, let's make a pact. If you happen to run into me somewhere, please grab my left hand with the fake diamond and exclaim loudly with a smile, "What a lovely ring, Rachel—so big and so sparkly!"

I'll reply with a wink, "Thank you, girlfriend! Aren't you the sweetest!"

Really, no one else needs to know.

1

Always RSVP

Revealing the Secret to Responding to God

Everyone has a story. Everyone chooses to ignore God, (re)define God, or search for God and respond to Him as He truly is. I've done all three.

When I was growing up, my family attended church in a brown brick building with stained-glass windows and bright red carpet. The sanctuary smelled faintly of wood. I'm surprised I remember the smell; we weren't there often—a few times a year.

I don't remember much about going to church other than feeling embarrassed by my mother's singing. We rarely went, but each time we did Mom sat us front and center, and then she sang as loudly as she could. She sang with passion, but she couldn't carry a tune with a U-Haul. Being from the South I'm required to follow that criticism with "bless her heart." (So let it be noted here that I blessed my momma's can't-sing-a-lick heart.)

I listened to the pastor's sermons, but I didn't understand much about the subject matter. From what I could gather, God was good and He didn't do bad things. So I concluded that if I wanted God to like me I, too, needed to be good and not do anything bad. Being a proper Southern girl, I very much wanted God to like me.

I thought believing in God and trying to do the right thing was what church was all about. I didn't realize that—because Jesus lived, died, and rose—I could have a dynamic relationship with the God of the universe and He would delight in empowering me to live well. Instead, I assumed it took willpower. Like a diet or a marathon.

Glimpses of Revelation

When I was twelve, my mother called me into her room and patted the edge of the bed. I sat down beside her. With an unsettled look on her face, she revealed she'd been diagnosed with breast cancer. The room started to spin, splintering my carefree world within its centrifugal force.

She explained something about cells and masts. Then she braced me for the likelihood that the treatments would cause her hair to fall out. That did it. I ran from the room crying inconsolably. My momma, sick, without her pretty auburn hair? It was too much for a tweenager to take in. I might have been only twelve at the time, but I understood the importance of big hair to Southern women.

During the months of cancer treatments that followed we went to church more often. About this time our church employed a new minister, and I really liked him. I understood more of his sermons, perhaps because I was desperate, or maybe because I was growing up. All I know is I sensed something stirring in a dormant chamber of my heart.

I asked Mom to buy me a Bible; she did. I sat on the floor one Saturday, sunlight streaming through my window, and read through Genesis. (OK, I might have skimmed a little bit.) Then I skipped to the middle—because I'd never read a book this long—and read through Matthew, Mark, and part of Luke. Then I skipped to Revelation to find out how the book ended.

I don't know if you've spent much time in Revelation, but it isn't exactly light reading material. Challenging concepts make it difficult to grasp, especially for a clueless tween with no decoder ring. I closed the book, remembering the stories about Jesus. He lived doing good, which reconfirmed my notion that I had to be good and do good to make heaven's invitation list. I'd finally made a Jesus-sighting, but I was still missing His point. I didn't hear His message of mercy.

I set out to be and do good. I unloaded the dishwasher without being asked. I invited less-popular kids to sit at my lunch table. I even said "yes ma'am," and "no sir" to my teachers. But inevitably something would happen to throw me off my good game. Someone would insult me, something would depress me, or some boy would pass a note my way.

After a year or so of mastectomy recovery and radiation treatments, my mother's cancer went into remission. Things returned to normal around our home. Sadly, the preacher I liked so well left to pastor another church, and my interest in the things of God faded as my interest in the things of my peers grew. I didn't give God much thought during my high school years, preferring to focus on fashion, sports, boys, and music.

Halfway through my freshman year of college, my brother called to tell me Mom had again been diagnosed with cancer. This time, it was a brain tumor. His words sank into my own brain, creating a mass of stress and fret.

One night, I lay alone in my dorm room trying to sleep when I thought I saw Jesus standing in the corner. He didn't say anything; He just looked at me, His arms extended toward me. He looked just as He did in the statues you see in old churches—long brown hair and white flowing robe. I wasn't sure if I was dreaming or hallucinating, but I decided it meant that my mom was going to be OK.

Turned out, the tumor was inoperable. The doctors resorted to chemotherapy and radiation, but I could tell they didn't think it'd work. I spent my spring semester driving the two hours back and forth between college and home. By exam week I was sick with a sinus infection, probably stress-induced. I'd take an exam, drag myself back to my room and sleep, then stagger—coughing and sniffling—to the next test. At the end of the week, I lugged myself home.

Hope Deferred

That Sunday, Mother's Day, I visited Mom at the cancer center, determined to keep a smile on my face and do my best to cheer her up. I didn't want her worrying about me. I purchased a sweet card and wrote, "Thank you for being my mom." When I arrived, the nurse told me I couldn't enter her room because I was sick.

I still remember the sterile feeling of the cold, hard floor in the hall outside her room, where I sat and cried. *But it's Mother's Day,* my mind protested between sobs, *but she's dying anyway....* Even today, the memory stings my eyes with tears.

A few days later I was better, but Mom had worsened. She came home from the cancer center with hospice care. A couple days after that, she couldn't respond to me beyond raising her eyebrows at the sound of my voice. Panic set in as I realized I was losing contact. She was sliding away, and I was powerless to stop the inevitable.

Later that evening, my dad and I went out to grab dinner, leaving Mom under my grandmother's watch. As we returned, I spotted a police car parked out front—and I knew. I ran to the bedroom to find my beautiful, vibrant mom lying lifeless.

She was gone. I was seventeen.

That night my life passed before me. Not my history with my mom, but my future without her. Where my prospects once looked promisingly bright, I now saw a haze of uncertainty.

I cried on the shoulder of a family friend. Gasping for breath and wiping away tears, I questioned, "What will I do when it comes time to graduate and my mom isn't there to pin on my cap and clap? Or when I set out on my own and I don't have my mom to advise me? What happens when I get married, and have babies, and I don't have a mom to help me?"

Placing her hands on my trembling shoulders, she stared into my moist eyes. "When those times come, Rachel, God will make sure you are taken care of." She spoke the words with enough certainty that I resolved to believe her.

Filing that promise away in my heart, I held on to the hope that God would somehow become a mother to me. I had nothing else to cling to. My dad and brothers argued over Mom's will, then went their separate ways. I didn't just lose my mom; I lost my whole family that May.

Coming Undone

In the fall I headed back to college, where I majored in journalism. I spent weekends trying to drown my sorrows at fraternity parties. I recall stumbling home one evening and walking into my closet, where I caught sight of one of my mom's sweaters. My knees buckled beneath me as heavy sobs ensued. I realized the party life wasn't fixing anything; it was an insufficient distraction. But I didn't know how else to find relief.

My junior year I met a corduroy-clad young professor with uncommon wisdom and peace. He taught two of my classes, scheduled back-to-back. As the weather turned cool and leaves crunched underfoot, we'd walk across campus together from one class to the other. I learned he was a Christian. He felt like a safe place. I couldn't remember the last time I'd felt that way around anybody.

I found myself telling him about my mom, my fractured family, and my uneasiness about the future. I asked him questions about his faith. He answered convincingly, and when the semester ended, he invited me to his church.

Inside that prefab metal building I witnessed vibrancy. Those people possessed hope, joy, and peace, all of which I coveted. I learned about Jesus and how His shed blood washes away my sin and unites me with God—even though I don't deserve such kindness.

I discovered God doesn't just want me to be good, He wants me to be *in Him*—hand in hand, heart to heart. I realized it isn't just a matter of willpower and proper performance He's after, but a growing relationship through which He'll shoulder most of the burden to make me vibrant. Yahweh so desires that I bear His image, I learned, He will transform me into His likeness through His Spirit. He can make the most tarnished Southern belle glorious. In fact, in Him my purpose is found and fulfilled. In coming to Him I'd become a daughter, a sister, a friend, and a bride. All in Him, and all to Him.

After attending church two Sundays, I responded to this divine truth. I walked to the front, acknowledged my need for Jesus, and handed Him the jumbled mess of my broken heart. I asked Him to forgive me, clear the haze, and untangle my knotted-up hopes and dreams.

Inside a priceless decoder ring, God inscribed my initials with an eternal beam of light. In the instant I responded to Christ's call, I became a beloved daughter of the Most High God and a member of His Yahweh Sisterhood.

The Favor of a Reply Is Requested

You and I need a jeweler's loupe of sorts to see the secrets Yahweh wants to reveal to us—indeed to see Yahweh Himself. Our basic eyesight needs some spiritual amplification. We need a divine ointment to anoint our eyes for the task.

Remember that Greek word *musterion,* meaning a sacred secret revealed by God? Its root word is *muo,* which means locked up or shut, as in eyes that are closed. In Revelation 3:17–18 Jesus told the people of the church at Laodicea that, although they didn't realize it, they were spiritually blind. Their eyes were locked shut and could not see God. They were neither seeing nor responding. Jesus counseled them, "Buy from me ... salve to anoint your eyes, so that you may see" (v. 18 ESV). Jesus affords us the ability to see, hear, understand, and respond to God. Only Jesus can provide that divine salve we need.

In Matthew 5, we find Jesus perched on the side of a mountain near the ancient city of Capernaum to preach. Massive crowds
gathered to watch and hear what He had to say. Some in the crowd
followed Jesus; they had already opened themselves to His teaching. Others desperately sought a miracle or healing. A few counted
themselves Jesus' enemies. Others showed up out of curiosity. They'd
heard the rumors and came to decide for themselves if Jesus was a
fake, a prophet, or a Savior.

Jesus gazed across the mountainside at the congregation of
people. Many eyed Him skeptically, wondering if they would
see something that proved a connection to God. He told them,
"Blessed are the pure in heart, for they will see God" (Matt. 5:8
NIV). A pure heart; an authentic heart; a humble, believing heart
open to Jesus' teaching—that's the currency that buys the salve
to allow our eyes to see God. That's what enables us to respond to
God. Lacking it, many heard Jesus' words without understanding
Him or watched His moves without realizing they were staring
into the face of Yahweh.

God's gals understand that only Jesus can open the eyes of a
woman's heart, cleansing them pure enough to see and respond to
Yahweh. Jesus says in John 14:6, "I am the way, the truth, and the
life. No one can come to the Father except through me." Did you
catch the secret Jesus reveals here? He said *He's* the only way to God,
the full embodiment of truth, and the only source of vibrant, lasting
life. Jesus is the way we want to go, the truth we need to know, and
the eternal life that we crave. You just can't get to God without going
through Jesus. Jesus is our way to God, and God's way to us.

Jesus is who God wants us to respond to.

All religions do not lead to heaven, despite popular opinion (John 3:3). God is wise beyond wise and has a purpose for everything He does, and He designed salvation in such a way that believing in God is not sufficient. We must also believe in His Son, who ushers us to Yahweh and shows us how to live His way.

So our membership in the Yahweh Sisterhood—our becoming a daughter of God—happens at Christ's invitation to follow Him. You cannot buy, earn, or bluff your way in. You must be invited—*and you have been.* God's own hand addressed your invitation some two thousand years ago, at the desk of the cross, on the parchment of Christ's body, in the ink of His blood.

Have you RSVP'd?

A year of high school French enables me to inform you RSVP stands for *"répondez s'il vous plaît."* It means "please respond" … *don't put it off … don't wait and see … say you'll join me!*

If you've never responded to Jesus' invitation to come to God through Him, now is the time. Don't wait for tomorrow. Don't put it off until you get your act together—RSVP right now through prayer. Receive the gift of forgiveness offered through Jesus, and ask God to take charge of your life and future. Receive your divine decoder ring. Tomorrow may be too late. Be Jesus' guest today.

Guest List

In Jesus' day, a person throwing a soiree sent out servants to issue invitations to the guests and gather their responses. Invitations noted the day of the gathering but not the hour. The hour depended on when everything was ready.

Once everything was ready on party day, servants again went out to call in the guests. Those who'd said they'd come were expected to be dressed, ready, and waiting that day. When the servant knocked on their door, they were to head immediately for the banquet room.

This scenario mirrors what happens in the spiritual realm. God sent His Son and Servant Jesus to issue our invitation on the cross. Those who accept are born anew spiritually—then expected and empowered to live in such a way that they are ready for the day Jesus will return, calling us to God's heavenly banqueting table.

Though we don't know the day or the hour, we will be ushered to a great wedding feast, the marriage banquet for Jesus and His bride. Jesus' bride is the church, meaning you and me—all who have RSVP'd to His invitation.

I read about this feast in the book of Revelation that day in my room. What I couldn't grasp fully back then now sets my heart aflutter in a way that nothing else can. I am loved, chosen, adopted, prepared, and betrothed—to the King of Glory. You are too! The wildest thing about this Yahweh Sisterhood? We're all engaged to the same Man—Jesus—yet no one seems to mind.

You and I must RSVP and ready ourselves for our heavenly wedding day. The rest of the divine secrets in this book will purify and prepare us to take our Groom's hand as He replaces our decoder ring with a wedding band. I don't want to miss it. Nor do I want to get there and find myself underdressed and unprepared.

Understanding and responding to the twelve divine secrets that follow—internalizing and enacting them—will keep us dressed and ready for the future party. While simply responding to the cross secures our seat at the grand banqueting table, keeping these secrets assures us that our heavenly Groom will look on us with utter delight.

My fellow belles, have you saved the date? Because a wedding feast looms on the celestial calendar. It's part of your story. And savvy Yahweh Sisters are always dressed and ready for a party!

A Garden Wedding

Twenty days after I graduated college, I had my own wedding feast. I married that young professor, Southern style, in a garden surrounded by azalea bushes in full bloom, three-hundred-year-old oaks dripping with Spanish moss, and swans swimming on the lake behind. It was gorgeous.

God not only adopted this lonely girl into His heavenly family, He placed me into Rick's earthly family. He presented me with three sisters-in-law and countless Sisters-in-Christ. I learned the truthful relevance of Psalm 68; it became the story of my life:

> Sing praises to God and to his name!
> Sing loud praises to him who rides the clouds.
> His name is the LORD—rejoice in his presence!
>
> Father to the fatherless, defender of widows—
>   this is God, whose dwelling is holy.
> God places the lonely in families;
>   he sets the prisoners free and gives them joy.
> (Ps. 68:4–6)

He's a Father to the fatherless, and I can testify He's a mother to the motherless as well. God has guided me, protected me, comforted me, taught me, and provided for me. He also untangled my hopes and fears and brought me the joyful desires of my heart.

So now you'll find me in church each week, singing praises to Yahweh and His great name. Oh, and I sing rather quietly when I praise Him in public. It's not that I'm not extremely thankful—I am. It's not that I don't like to sing—I do. And it has nothing to do with embarrassing memories from my church past in that brown brick building with the red carpet.

Truth is, I sing every stinkin' bit as off-key as my momma did. *Shhh, don't tell anyone.* Sisters stick together, right?

But you can go ahead and bless my heart over that vocal deficit. I need all the help I can get.

BIBLE STUDY

1. Check out this parable Jesus told about a man throwing a feast:

> A man sitting at the table with Jesus exclaimed, "What a blessing it will be to attend a banquet in the Kingdom of God!"

> Jesus replied with this illustration: "A man prepared a great feast and sent out many invitations. When all was ready,

he sent his servant around to notify the guests that it was time for them to come. But they all began making excuses. One said he had just bought a field and wanted to inspect it, so he asked to be excused. Another said he had just bought five pair of oxen and wanted to try them out. Another had just been married, so he said he couldn't come.

"The servant returned and told his master what they had said. His master was angry and said, 'Go quickly into the streets and alleys of the city and invite the poor, the crippled, the lame, and the blind.' After the servant had done this, he reported, 'There is still room for more.' So his master said, 'Go out into the country lanes and behind the hedges and urge anyone you find to come, so that the house will be full. For none of those I invited first will get even the smallest taste of what I had prepared for them.'" (Luke 14:15–24)

What struck you when the people in Jesus' story made excuses for not being prepared to attend? List the things that preoccupied them.

What excuses do you make for not responding to Christ, or not living "dressed and ready"?

2. Read about the coming wedding feast in Revelation 19:6–10. What does it say about the bride (you) and her wedding dress?

3. Next time you throw a bash at your plantation, Jesus offers this advice for planning the guest list:

> Then he turned to his host. "When you put on a luncheon or a banquet," he said, "don't invite your friends, brothers, relatives, and rich neighbors. For they will invite you back, and that will be your only reward. Instead, invite the poor, the crippled, the lame, and the blind. Then at the resurrection of the righteous, God will reward you for inviting those who could not repay you." (Luke 14:12–14)

That's precisely what God did when He created the Yahweh Sisterhood. He sent out invitations welcoming every one of us to His supper club. The glass slipper fits each gal here. Everyone gets the rose. The King of Glory doesn't require designer gowns or shiny black limos for us to dine with Him. What a relief!

In the space below, write a thank-you note to your King.

Dear Jesus,

_____

_____

_____

_____

_____

2

Know When to Pay Retail

Revealing the Secret Cost of Following Christ

A potent swath of sunlight cut past the curtains through the stale air. I kept my knees slightly bent and the handheld microphone back a bit further than normal so a sudden shift in the room wouldn't send me careening off-balance. I'd spoken in classrooms, churches, hotels, and retreat centers, but never before in a cocktail lounge on a cruise ship.

I was leading a Christian women's retreat on a Caribbean cruise with recording artist Gwen Smith. In case you're fancying it quite glamorous to speak on a cruise, let me put that notion to rest. After swallowing Dramamine with breakfast, Gwen and I watched the ocean go by each day through the windows of the ship's darkened lounge where we set up, sound checked, rehearsed, and delivered multiple sessions before breaking down in time for a late dinner. No doubt there are worse places to work, and we thoroughly enjoyed our time with the women we were serving, but it was still work.

Each night Gwen and I returned to our stateroom and melted into our twin-size berths. We were both looking forward to the few hours of free time we'd spend in port in Nassau. With not enough time to snorkel, we decided on the next best thing—shopping. Once the ship docked, Gwen laced up her tennis shoes, I donned my flip-flops, and we headed ashore in search of the Straw Market.

The Straw Market is a staple of Nassau tourism. Rows of local vendor booths sit crammed together under a large tent. It's hot, loud, crowded, and chaotic. Merchants yell at you from down the aisle to come look at their wares, and some use interesting tactics. One woman kept calling, "Sexy lady, over here! Hey, sexy lady, jewelry for you!" For a long time I ignored her, assuming she couldn't possibly be talking to this thirtysomething mother of two in flip-flops. She was.

It's not a shopping experience for the mild-mannered. You're expected to bargain unless you want to overpay by as much as half. You'll see women weaving palm and sisal leaves into souvenir baskets and dolls. You'll also find them aggressively hawking shell jewelry, tourist T-shirts, and knockoff designer handbags. The latter excited Gwen.

Many vendors offer the same item, so you walk the aisles seeking who you can talk down the most for what you want. Gwen found a brown "Gucci" handbag sporting the trademark double "G" logo. She went row by row through the market tempting sellers to price it lower than forty dollars. An authentic Gucci bag at an upscale store in the States could easily run one thousand dollars.

The more designer-looking bags I walked by, the more I thought I might want one. I examined a few, braved the waters at negotiating a price (and I *hate* haggling prices), but ultimately decided to pass. Gwen got her "Gucci" bag and a matching wallet. As the ship pulled out of port and we went back to work, I wondered if I'd made the right decision or missed an opportunity for a great bargain.

The Price

My parents owned a chain of Hallmark stores, so I'm well versed in the practice of retail markup. Most gift items in our stores were marked a flat 50 percent over wholesale. However, like the booths in the Straw Market, retail markup amounts can vary among industries. Small appliance manufacturers typically apply a 30 percent markup, for instance, while clothing is often marked up as much as 100 percent. Most new cars carry only a 5 to 10 percent markup, but SUVs in their heyday carried a 25 percent markup. The diamond industry has one of the highest retail markups at 300 to 800 percent!

Is it ever a good idea to pay retail price? Not all markup is profit since the business owner must pay operating expenses and employees. Plus, there are times in a gal's life when she just has to have something, even if it's not on sale. Occasionally I pay full price with careless abandon. But it makes me downright giddy to find an item offered at deep discount, so I usually wait for sales.

My pulse quickens at the sight of a clearance sign. From deep within, a pleasurable urgency wells up, compelling me to find a treasure on that rack. It's the modern equivalent of hunting and gathering ... the twenty-first-century thrill of the hunt. My husband doesn't find shopping thrilling at all. I tell him that's because men just buy, while women *shop*. Rick likes to claim I save us more money than he earns with all the treasures I find.

Is any treasure really worth emptying our wallets ... and then draining our bank accounts too? According to Jesus, YES.

The Treasure

Shortly after telling His disciples there are secrets in the kingdom of God, Jesus told several parables designed to reveal something of the nature of this kingdom. While three gospel writers use the words "kingdom of God," Jews were trained not to write Yahweh's name, out of respect. Therefore, Matthew uses the term "kingdom of heaven" to refer to places where God's reign is discernible or apparent. Nowhere was it more apparent than in the life of Christ. It's still discernible today in the lives of His followers.

A parable is a story used to compare or contrast an earthly situation with a spiritual reality. In chapter 13, Matthew records Jesus telling this parable:

> The Kingdom of Heaven is like a treasure that a man discovered hidden in a field. In his excitement, he hid it again and sold everything he owned to get enough money to buy the field—and to get the treasure, too! (v. 44)

When I first read this, I thought this guy was deceptive to hide the treasure and pay the field owner less than the field's true worth. I expected Jesus to use this story to teach us to be scrupulously honest in all our dealings. Yet Jesus makes him the hero of the tale.

In the absence of banks, people hid their assets the best they could, often in the ground. They ran the risk of someone else discovering it, and the risk of forgetting exactly where it was buried. If those with knowledge of the treasure died suddenly, the treasure could lie hidden for generations until someone found it.

So, "finders keepers" for Jesus' hero? Not exactly. The man didn't take the found treasure; he put it back and paid the asking price for the field. In fact, he sold everything he owned to buy it.

While initially critical of the treasure hider, I realized I've done basically the same thing. Yesterday, in fact. While in the mall, I happened upon an end-of-season sale, a heady experience where you get to take an additional 50 percent off the lowest marked price.

After diligent searching through the handbag department, I found it—my treasure. A purse in just the right color, in just the right size, with just the right amount of bling on the buckle. Starting price was forty dollars, recently marked down to twenty dollars, and with the additional percent off, it'd only be ten dollars. (I can't believe my husband doesn't find this thrilling!)

Before heading to check out, I wondered, *What if other stores are having equally fabulous sales today and I can find a more fabulous bag?* I suddenly felt the need to comparison shop. So I took my treasure and placed it on the top shelf well above sight line for safekeeping. For good measure, I then pushed it as far back as my five-foot-two frame would allow. I made it unlikely anyone else would notice it before I returned.

Later I recovered my treasure from its hidden spot and purchased it. It's lovely, and the bling on the buckle makes me smile. So I'm not so different from the hero in Jesus' tale with my questionable, sneaky, treasure-hiding impulses. When I happen upon something valuable to me, I also go to lengths to lay hold of it, to possess and protect it.

How much more should I be motivated to lay hold of the kingdom of God?

The difference between Jesus' field-buying hero and me is that I spent ten bucks for my treasure. That's not much of a stretch. He, however, sold everything he owned to lay hold of that field. This took time, effort, commitment, and guts. He literally sold out for his treasure. Matthew Henry, in his classic commentary on the Bible, writes, "Those who discern this treasure in the field, and value it aright, will never be easy till they have made it their own upon any terms."[1]

Jesus follows up the treasure-in-a-field parable with a second, similar parable. Again illustrating the value of the kingdom of God, Jesus compares it to a pearl of surpassing beauty and quality:

> Again, the Kingdom of Heaven is like a pearl
> merchant on the lookout for choice pearls. When he
> discovered a pearl of great value, he sold everything
> he owned and bought it! (Matt. 13:45-46)

Jesus compared His kingdom to treasure and then to jewelry—my God resonates with my own heart!

The difference between these two parables is that in the first, the man simply stumbled upon the treasure. We don't see him out trolling for treasure in every field. He's not at the famed Christie's auction house. He's not standing in line on *Antiques Roadshow* or scouring eBay. He's an everyday guy who happened upon a treasure and realized its worth. An everyday bloke giving his all for his chance at something great when the opportunity arose.

The field buyer's story tears down my tendency to think living sold out for God is only expected of monks, scribes, nuns, pastors, or missionaries. Nope, this sold-out living—and the treasures it brings—is for any and every Yahweh Sister. It's for each gal willing to pay the price in her daily life to follow Christ. No great spiritual background or seminary degree is required. It's for bank tellers, kindergarten teachers, nurses, cafeteria workers, hairstylists, corporate executives, college students, stay-at-home moms, and grandmothers alike.

The pearl merchant, unlike the field buyer, actively searched for his treasure. His focus was finding that superb pearl, and he made it his daily quest. I admire him—ready to invest all he had once he found a treasure worthy of such sacrifice. He knew what was valuable, and he was going after it.

Both these characters recognized the worth of the treasures they encountered and literally dropped everything to obtain them. They boldly invested all, and were happy with that decision. Matthew Henry writes, "All the children of men are busy …; one would be rich, another would be honourable, another would be learned; but the most are imposed upon, and take up with counterfeits for pearls…. Jesus Christ is a Pearl of great price …; in having him, we have enough to make us happy here and for ever."[2]

The Cost

Neither of these parables should be interpreted to suggest we can buy our salvation, for salvation is a free gift. However, they suggest there is a price to pay to lay full hold of the treasures of God's kingdom. I consider it the price of *abandon*.

When we first come to Christ He accepts us as we are—warts, sins, selfish compulsions, and all. Soon we discover that because Jesus loves us, He doesn't want to leave us this way. He wants to disciple us and show us the way to the treasure, but that requires some focus and a surrendered commitment on our end. In other words, we must abandon ourselves to Him and sell out to the one true thing worth selling out to.

When I first became a believer, my friends challenged my new faith. They questioned my God and His lavish grace. They asked me questions like, "So if an ax murderer confesses his sins and prays to accept Christ minutes before his execution, he could go to heaven, and God would take him?"

"Yes, that's possible. He could be forgiven and saved despite the awful things he had done," I'd reply. This visibly upset them. They felt it unjust and didn't want any part of a God who would allow someone else who'd spent their whole life serving God to stand side-by-side in heaven with an ax murderer.

I understood their disappointment. Honestly, I felt it a bit too. I didn't know then what I know now—that the person who "pays retail" by serving God with abandon receives a tremendous amount of blessing as they walk this earth with Him, and even more as they step from here into eternity.

Another man, not just a character in a parable this time and one much less given to abandon, had opportunity to sell all he owned to grasp the treasure of the kingdom of God:

> Once a religious leader asked Jesus this question:
> "Good teacher, what should I do to get eternal life?"

"Why do you call me good?" Jesus asked him. "Only God is truly good. But as for your question, you know the commandments: 'Do not commit adultery. Do not murder. Do not steal. Do not testify falsely. Honor your father and mother.'"

The man replied, "I've obeyed all these commandments since I was a child."

"There is still one thing you lack," Jesus said. "Sell all you have and give the money to the poor, and you will have treasure in heaven. Then come, follow me."

But when the man heard this, he became sad because he was very rich. (Luke 18:18–23)

The guy approached Jesus asking what he could do to secure eternal life for himself. Jesus' response seems strangely off topic: "Why do you call me good? Only God is good." Jesus is actually cutting to the chase here. He's throwing out a clue about who He is. And He is pointing out, since only God is good, men and women don't qualify for the label. We're certainly not good enough to earn eternal life no matter which rules we manage to keep.

The young religious leader doesn't get the implied point. He didn't have the spiritual ears to hear it. Next, we see why. Displaying his pride, he announces he has adequately kept all these commandments since childhood. Jesus doesn't argue with him, though we know the Bible says no one is faultless but Christ. Instead, Jesus gives him what he asked for, an action to carry out—the action of full abandonment.

Jesus essentially says to him, *If you really want to enter into true life, sell out to Me with careless abandon. Give up your allegiance to all your stuff and your power, and content yourself in walking daily with Me.*

Here's this rich guy's really big chance. He's staring straight at a treasure greater than anything he owned, and it could be his. Only he didn't recognize it. He didn't have the eyes to see its worth. He misjudged the value of the kingdom of God and settled for his stuff—a counterfeit pearl.

The young man walked away sad but unyielding:

> Jesus watched him go and then said to his disciples, "How hard it is for rich people to get into the Kingdom of God! It is easier for a camel to go through the eye of a needle than for a rich person to enter the Kingdom of God!"
>
> Those who heard this said, "Then who in the world can be saved?"
>
> He replied, "What is impossible from a human perspective is possible with God." (Luke 18:24–27)

Jesus points out that wealth provides a sense of security, comfort, and pride that can cloud our spiritual vision, causing us to miss the worth of the kingdom of God. This shakes me to my core when I get honest about how much time I spend pursing creature comforts instead of the treasure of Christ.

The disciples and witnesses to this encounter wondered aloud who could be saved if that rich, young, powerful religious leader—who had purportedly kept every commandment—couldn't be. Jesus assured that salvation will always be impossible for man to earn, but God will give it to those who yield to Him. Don't miss this—then Jesus let the disciples know that *even more* will be given to those who not only yield, but wholeheartedly sell out to Him with abandon:

> Peter said, "We've left our homes to follow you."

> "Yes," Jesus replied, "and I assure you that everyone who has given up house or wife or brothers or parents or children, for the sake of the Kingdom of God, will be repaid many times over in this life, as well as receiving eternal life in the world to come." (Luke 18:28–30)

The Worth

Did you catch that promise? Eternal life *and* repayment many times over for those who pay the cost to yield all for Christ. This motivates me to examine my heart and see if I'm barely yielding, or really abandoning myself to God. Am I the pearl merchant or the rich, young ruler?

I sometimes ask myself before God that if I had to choose between Christ and my home, would I choose Christ? If I had to choose between Christ and my family, could I choose Christ? What about my bank account or retirement account? What about my health—my vision, hearing, or ability to walk? Would I willingly give any of these up to gain the treasures of the kingdom of God? What if God allowed me to be falsely accused and I lost my reputation or my ministry, or I went to jail unjustly? Would I still serve Him? I feel the need to settle these things in my heart before God, regardless of whether it will ever come to that.

The truth is that there is no appropriate or reasonable place to draw a line with God. Sometimes I have to keep praying until I can willingly place the things most dear to me, mainly my husband and children, on the altar of God and say with conviction, "Not my will but Yours be done." In these moments of quiet clarity, I realize the kingdom of God is worth everything I have and much more.

Perhaps like me, after reading these parables, you're feeling motivated to sell out to God and lay hold of His kingdom. Before rushing out to place a for-sale sign in our front yards or car windows, let's start by asking God what He would require of us this day. Then follow through on it. He may ask us to sell our homes, or He may just ask us to cross the street and take soup to a sick neighbor.

Through these parables, Jesus reveals the paramount *worth* of the kingdom of God, and the secret reality that anything we give or lose as a result of following Him is more than a bargain for what we'll receive in return.

The Lesson

My phone rang two weeks after Gwen and I returned home from the cruise. "Rachel, it broke," Gwen announced with a mix of disbelief and frustration. "I'm standing in a shoe store where I planned to find some shoes to go with my new bag, and the strap just ripped right off. The purse fell to the ground and spilled everything in it." I commiserated with my friend over her not-worth-it purse. As we hung up, I knew I'd made the right decision that day in the Straw Market.

Some treasures are counterfeits—cheap imitations—like Gwen's fake Gucci purse. They call out to you in the marketplace, attracting you, tempting you, flattering you. Other things—secret, sacred things—wait quietly to be discovered and seized with gusto.

I'm a die-hard bargain shopper, but Jesus has taught me that one thing is worth my all, worth paying retail for: the kingdom of God and its King, Jesus. The gospel of Christ is more than a gracious offer of saving grace; it's also a call for surrendered abandon and supreme loyalty.

Yahweh Sisters, remember that our salvation is free, but not cheap. And our abandon to God is costly, but worth every penny. Selling out to God truly pays divinely.

BIBLE STUDY

1. Which character do you identify with most: the stumbling field-buyer, the searching pearl merchant, or the rich, young ruler? Explain.

2. Read Matthew 16:24–27:

Then Jesus said to his disciples, "If anyone would come after me, he must deny himself and take up his cross and follow me. For whoever wants to save his life will lose it, but whoever loses his life for me will find it. What good will it be for a man if he gains the whole world, yet forfeits his soul? Or what can a man give in exchange for his soul? For the Son of Man is going to come in his Father's glory with his angels, and then he will reward each person according to what he has done." (NIV)

What do you think Jesus means when He says, "If anyone would come after me"?

3. In that same verse, what does Jesus mean by denying yourself, taking up your cross, and following Him? What would this look like in your daily life?

For some ideas see Matthew 6:16–18 on fasting, Matthew 10:37–39 on family, Matthew 10:42 on the innocent and needy, 1 Peter 4:12–13 on suffering, and 1 Corinthians 13:3–7 on love.

4. What is God asking you to sacrifice, give, or do today?

Will you resist or surrender?

5. According to the last verse in the Matthew 16 passage quoted, what awaits you in the future?

6. In Matthew 16:25, Jesus reveals a God-sized secret. In your own words, what is it?

7. Now take out your Bible and read about a Yahweh Sister in Matthew 26:6–13 who recognized the true worth of Jesus.

This gal doesn't just spritz a little perfume behind Jesus' ear and save the rest for another occasion. She pours it on with reckless abandon. Furthermore, this isn't like a sixty-dollar bottle of Chanel No. 5 to you or me. Bible scholars estimate this perfume's worth at more than a couple years' wages!

Witnesses deemed her actions impractical, maybe even ungodly, because she didn't sell the perfume and give the proceeds to the poor. Tell of a time you did something in obedience to or in honor of God, only to be thought foolish by others.

8. Record here, from the second half of Matthew 26:10, how Jesus views actions of radical worship or obedience.

9. According to verse 12 of her story in Matthew 26, what role did her action of abandon play in God's plan?

10. The fact that you and I are reading about her today illustrates God's desire to reward those who abandon themselves to Him. What was Jesus' promised reward to her?

11. This Yahweh Sister made a costly sacrifice and probably felt in her heart it wasn't enough to match Jesus' worth. Now read the next paragraph in Matthew 26:14–16. What price did this next follower of Jesus place on Christ's worth? How does your own heart react to that?

12. Friend, what is Jesus worth in your eyes? What about in your actions?

3

Kill your Competition

Revealing the Secret Power of Humility

I had dinner one evening with someone you might consider famous: Ruth Graham, youngest daughter of evangelist Billy Graham. Several years ago she spoke at a fund-raising banquet for our local crisis pregnancy center. One of my husband's colleagues affiliated with the center asked him to emcee the event. I got to tag along.

Despite the fact that I find my husband articulate and entertaining in front of a microphone, I didn't consider the event the primary thing on my calendar that day. I had already spent the majority of the day at the same hotel attending a different event, a small conference for pastors' wives. I'd volunteered to assist the speaker, pass out handouts, and work the resource table.

After the pastors' wives conference, I went in the bathroom and slipped into a black skirt before heading to the dinner. I wouldn't make anyone's best-dressed list, but I deemed myself dressy enough to pass for banquet attire. I assumed I'd be sitting in the back unnoticed. After all, Rick was the one on stage that night, not me.

Entering the ballroom, I offered my name at the registration table. Since I was noted on their roster as wife of the emcee, someone led me to the front of the room, past a couple hundred people already seated at tables. I was suddenly wishing I'd dressed better.

They pointed to a round table next to the stage—the head table. I stared in disbelief at my name on a place card there. Even more unexpected, the place card next to mine read "Ruth Graham." Moments later, Ruth emerged from a side door. Someone—I have no idea who—introduced us, and she took her seat beside me. Ruth Graham, a part of twentieth-century evangelical "royalty," sat down to my left.

Most any other day, I might have panicked a little. Insecurity might have slithered its way up my underdressed torso, wrapped itself around my unadorned neck, attempting a choke hold. Or, my pride might have worried about measuring up, impressing, being memorable—acting like I belonged at the head table. But I'd spent the day worshipping and serving Jesus, and that made all the difference. Aware of His nearness, I felt secure and serene.

Ruth was good company, down-to-earth, and humble. That woman is one gracious Yahweh Sister. I know this because during her introduction, Rick accidently called her by her older sister Anne's name—*twice*. In Rick's defense, one of Anne's books had been laying on our kitchen table for a week, her name permeating his subconscious. He didn't notice his error, but everyone else in the room did. I looked sheepishly at Ruth with a shrug of apology. She leaned in and whispered reassuringly, "I get that all the time."

I wasn't so sure Ruth does get that all the time *when being intro-duced to speak at an event she's headlining.* Nonetheless, we laughed it off—she must've spent some time with Jesus that day too.

Other than referring to Ruth by the wrong name, Rick did a fine job. So did Ruth. By the end of her time behind the microphone that evening, we'd all spent a little time with Jesus.

Place Your Order

Speaking of dining with celebrities, I love the ice-breaker question "If you could have dinner one evening with anyone famous from the past, who would it be and why?" The most common answer I get when I ask new acquaintances this question is Jesus. But He is such a given that sometimes I outlaw that answer. Many will choose another Bible character—maybe an apostle or a prophet. But what if you had to choose from outside the Bible ... who would you dine with?

I'd choose C. S. Lewis. Lewis was an academic—an English pro-fessor at Oxford—as well as a writer. You may know him as author of The Chronicles of Narnia series. He created fantastical worlds with mythical creatures in Christian allegory.

But the fiction isn't what I value most from Lewis. With his pen, Lewis helps me kill my competition. (Sit tight, keep reading, and you'll see what I mean.) So that's one of the things we'd discuss at dinner over meatloaf. Englishmen like meatloaf, right?

The Competitive Spirit

I honed my competitive spirit for decades before ever reading a line of Lewis' work. In fact, I've been competing as long as I can remember: on a balance beam, in the classroom, on the track, behind the keyboard, in a gym, on the stage, in the kitchen, on committees, and in the workplace. I've competed for trophies, friends, boys, ribbons, praise, scholarships, jobs, opportunities, resources, attention, and respect.

Competition weaves through the very fabric of our society, from sports, to academics, to the free-market economy. Our culture embodies the survival of the fittest. "May the best man win," as the saying goes. Of course, women can be every bit as competitive as men. I certainly can.

Even if you've never participated in athletic competition or performed for a panel of judges, I suspect you've competed too. Even if only inside your own head. An attitude of competition causes us to worry about how we stack up against others—our desire is to be at or near the top. It makes us anxious about getting our share, especially of something that seems celebrated or limited. It's concerned with getting the credit—after all, recognition drives the competitive spirit.

At times we compete for fun. (Although things can get heated around my house over a friendly round of Uno or Scrabble!) Other times, we must compete to win to eke out a living. For example, if your start-up company doesn't succeed in grabbing a share of the market, you'll be out of a job.

Often, however, our competitive urge spews like molten lava out of the volcano of our unchecked pride—damaging precious things in its path, like family, friends, and the Yahweh Sisterhood. That's something Mr. Lewis taught me with his pen. He wrote:

> Now what I want you to get clear is that Pride is *essentially* competitive—is competitive by its very

nature—while the other vices are competitive only,
so to speak, by accident. Pride gets no pleasure out
of having something, only out of having more of it
than the next man.[1]

Sigh—how true. If I have only what the next person has, I feel ordinary. Ordinary doesn't stand out, doesn't win the prize, doesn't earn acclaim. Never mind that I might have enough. Or that I might have exactly as much as God knows I'm capable of handling well. My ego wants more—noticeably more—than the next gal.

Is it really so bad to want more, or to crave attention? I remember learning in college about "Maslow's Hierarchy of Needs." His theory stated that everyone needs food, clothing, shelter, and security. But once a gal's basic needs for food, shelter, and safety are met, he said everyone needs love, attention, and belonging. If Maslow is right, what's wrong with seeking to be noticed or even admired?

Mr. Lewis warned, "The vain person wants praise, applause, admiration, too much and is always angling for it."[2] "Too much" and "always angling" resonate as a fair description of me at times. So the problem lies, according to Lewis, not in the need for attention or even in our desire for greatness, but in the posturing and jockeying to grasp it for oneself. I think Jesus would agree with that, based on another story He told.

Take Your Seats

A prominent Pharisee invited Jesus and other religious leaders to a dinner party at his home. Don't assume these religious leaders desired to have dinner with Jesus for the same reasons you and I would.

They hoped to trick Him into breaking a religious law and arrest Him for it. The party took place on the Sabbath—a day of rest from work—and they'd invited a sick man to attend, expecting Jesus to do the work of healing him.

Jesus did exactly as expected, and then surprised them. He healed the man, asserting that showing compassion to someone in need did not violate God's Sabbath law any more than helping your young son up when he falls down. The experts, who had surely helped a child up on some Sabbath or another, groped for a counterargument but came up empty-handed. Jesus offered more wisdom, as He took them to task based on where they'd chosen to sit.

Dinner parties in Jesus' day took place at three large tables forming a flat-bottomed U-shape. The middle of the U remained open for servants to serve from, while guests reclined around the outer perimeter. The central seat was deemed a place of honor, and seats close to it were esteemed as well.

When Jesus noticed everyone at the party maneuvering for the seats of honor near the head of the table, He advised:

> "If you are invited to a wedding feast, don't always head for the best seat. What if someone more respected than you has also been invited? The host will say, 'Let this person sit here instead.' Then you will be embarrassed and will have to take whatever seat is left at the foot of the table!

> "Do this instead—sit at the foot of the table. Then when your host sees you, he will come and say,

'Friend, we have a better place than this for you!' Then you will be honored in front of all the other guests." (Luke 14:8–10)

Jesus' words poked at their pride. The same arrogance that drove them to seek the best seats for themselves also drove them to want to trap Jesus because He was gaining popularity among the people. And they all knew it. When pride raises its selfish head, it taints our every motivation and action. Pride pulls our focus inward. Our entire viewpoint shrinks down to the size of ourselves. We'll never see God that way.

Jesus' hypothetical story concluded with this kingdom secret, "For everyone who exalts himself will be humbled, and he who humbles himself will be exalted" (v. 11 NIV). Once again, a divine truth runs completely counter to worldly ways.

Sharpening Knives

When our pride swells, it becomes vanity. *I deserve better than this.* We seek status we do not merit, and function with an assumed autonomy we do not have. *I know best. I'll decide how my life should be.* Soon, we envy those who appear to have more than we do and disdain those who appear to be less than we are. *I don't want to sit by her; I want to sit with them.* And we plot our next move to advance our own position.

Sharpening our knives, with mouths watering for the next course, we grow grabby, arrogant, and insecure—all while remaining inconsiderate or even oblivious to those down the table who've yet to taste a crumb of what we just devoured. Yahweh Sisters, the cold fact of it is this: Pride and competition oppose humility and service.

Humility can be defined as the absence of excessive pride. In that sense, we can think of humility as what's left when our pretense is stripped away.

Or, we could take C. J. Mahaney's definition: "Humility is honestly assessing ourselves in light of God's holiness and our sinfulness."[3] Like Mahaney, I believe a clear view of God is a prerequisite for an accurate view of ourselves.

I also like the *HarperCollins Bible Dictionary* definition, which says humility is "a socially acknowledged claim to neutrality in the competition of life."[4]

How do we reach this state of humble neutrality? And won't we be trampled or miserable if we do?

Humility's Focus

The interesting thing about humility is it emerges or retreats depending on what we focus on. That's why we scramble to quickly change the channel when a feed-the-children commercial appears. Watching those commercials can radically and uncomfortably shift our focus from our desires—which the other commercials reinforce, by the way—to others' needs. That shift is deadly to our selfish position of entitlement. The more this shift in focus happens, the more our pretense is stripped down and humility emerges. For me that shift is often accompanied by a deep urge to move closer to the floor, onto my knees perhaps.

Humility comes as we orient our attention on God and on helping others. To find it, we must lift our gaze from our own navels, or from our perceived competition, to the kingdom of God. When we make this shift, our so-called competition becomes someone to help, someone to befriend, someone to pray for and serve in the name of Christ.

Let me give you the typical progression. We see a woman we admire. We set out to emulate her. Once we get fairly good at our imitation, we no longer want to match her, but top her. Our former role model just became our perceived competition. We slid from comparison, to coveting, to competing … degrading the Sisterhood in the process.

In helping our Sisters get ahead, rather than grasping for what we feel *we* deserve, we find a pleasure we missed with all our striving. In looking at Christ rather than ourselves, Lewis assured, "You will, in fact, be humble—delightedly humble, feeling the infinite relief of having for once got rid of all the silly nonsense about your own dignity which has made you restless and unhappy all your life."[5]

Mercy, that sounds inviting! According to Lewis, humbly bowing out of the competitive rat race of life doesn't make us losers, but winners. That's what Jesus was saying at the dinner party. Humble yourself, and God will lift you up. Exalt yourself in pride, and God will put you in your proper place. I'd much prefer to humble myself before God than be humbled by Him through my circumstances. I don't want to be made to move to the back row.

In God's upside-down kingdom, we bend down to go up. The quickest way to the front of the line is to let others in front of us. To become great, we serve. Humility—not power, talent, fortune, or fame—is currency in His kingdom.

I've known people who didn't grasp at attention or lunge for the primo seat. In contrast, they were always saying how lowly they were and how undeserving they were of any seat. It looked like humility and sounded like humility, yet they didn't strike me as humble, like I picture Jesus. Nor did they strike me as particularly blessed by God when I heard them talk. Have you known people like this?

I'd want to ask Lewis about this over a forkful of salad. In his classic book *Mere Christianity*, Lewis described the difference between true humility and false humility:

> Do not imagine that if you meet a really humble man he will be what most people call "humble" nowadays: he will not be a sort of greasy, smarmy person, who is always telling you that, of course, he is nobody. Probably all you will think about him is that he seemed a cheerful, intelligent chap who took a real interest in what *you* said to *him*. If you do dislike him it will be because you feel a little envious of anyone who seems to enjoy life so easily. He will not be thinking about humility: he will not be thinking about himself at all.[6]

What freedom there is in not having to think constantly about ourselves! Not posturing and positioning or worrying that we might miss out on something valuable. What relief rests in not having to worry about how we present ourselves or how we're perceived for the sake of popularity or upward mobility.

Lewis tells us and Jesus shows us the beauty of embracing downward mobility. Unexpected joy is found in bending our knee, bowing our heart, and humbly deferring to someone else for a change.

Isn't Meek Weak?

Jesus spoke of humility in His famous Beatitudes speech: "God blesses those people who are humble. The earth will belong to them!" (Matt. 5:5 CEV). Some translations use *meek* rather than *humble,* and I think that word is more misunderstood than *humble* tends to be.

Meek sounds lowly and weak. But it's not at all. It's controlled strength. It's power under restraint. It's self-control. Jesus is the perfect picture of this. Even as almighty God, He humbled Himself to take human form in order to take us out of sin.

I think about Satan tempting Jesus in the desert. He coaxed a fasting Jesus to satisfy His gastronomic cravings by changing stones into bread. I hear Satan hissing, *Go ahead, get what You want … take what You need … make it happen!* Satan also tempted Jesus by offering "the nations of the world and all their glory" (Matt. 4:8). He offered them in return for worship. *Do this one thing and the world can be Your oyster. Go for it!* Then he tempted Jesus to force God to do His bidding. He suggested Jesus jump from a cliff requiring angels to save Him. I can hear him hiss, *You continually serve God; let's see if He'll really ssserve You.*

Satan appealed to Jesus' sense of pride and strength, just as he appeals to ours today. However, Jesus had a bigger picture in mind—God's will and our need. His determination to serve outweighed any selfish desires Satan might have stirred in Him.

Jesus said, "God blesses those people who are humble. The earth will belong to them!" (5:5 CEV). In other words, those God can trust to possess their power without seeking selfish gain or doing others harm, He can trust to possess so much more—indeed the whole earth!

A few sentences later in that same sermon Jesus said, "God blesses those who work for peace, for they will be called the children of God" (v. 9). I love the way Eugene Peterson phrases this verse: "You're blessed when you can show people how to cooperate instead of compete or fight. That's when you discover who you really are, and your place in God's family" (MSG). Learning to cooperate rather than compete, I find myself at home and at peace in the Sisterhood of Christ.

Set Free

Michelangelo described his artistic process as pulling sculptures out of the rock. He said, "Every block of stone has a statue inside it, and it is the task of the sculptor to discover it." This Italian artist once noted, "I saw the angel in the marble and carved until I set him free."

Michelangelo helps me see that with the Holy Spirit chipping away the pride and vanity in my heart, I become evidence of the Artist's handiwork. I emerge from the rock His creation, the image He intends, the child of God He imagines. I become gloriously all I am meant to be. Perhaps that's what Jesus hoped the Pharisees would realize when He told them those who humble themselves will be exalted. The term *exalted* may be fuzzy in our thinking as well. It means "illustrious, glorious, or dignified." Think of it as being pulled from the rock by the Divine Artist.

The exalted life Jesus promises results from humble deference to God and others. It's a life illustrative of the kindness and mercy of God. The exalted life doesn't necessarily mean we'll have exalted circumstances, or an exalted earthly position. It has nothing to do with a corner office or our name in lights. It's about God bringing forth the real you, setting you free from the slavery of your own vanity and pride. It's about becoming a God-made, rather than a self-made, woman.

Perfect Humility

After studying Lewis' writings and Jesus' advice at the dinner party, I summed up what I need to remember like this: When I stop trying to create a life for myself, I find the life He creates for me. When I cease trying to make a name for myself—competing, grasping, pushing my way to the top—His name emerges through the actions of my life. And in that process I am lifted up for others to see, not me, but Him. At last I am truly dignified, finding pleasure in pleasing and displaying Him.

Lewis wrote:

> And that is enough to raise our thoughts to what may happen when the redeemed soul, beyond all hope and nearly beyond belief, learns at last that she has pleased Him whom she was created to please. There will be no room for vanity then. She will be free from the miserable illusion that it is her doing. With no taint of what we should now call self-approval she will most innocently rejoice in the

thing that God has made her to be, and the moment
which heals her old inferiority complex forever will
also drown her pride deeper than Prospero's book.
Perfect humility dispenses with modesty. If God is
satisfied with the work, the work may be satisfied
with itself; "it is not for her to bandy compliments
with her Sovereign."[7]

Now do you see why I'd choose to have dinner with this chap?

I spent years honing my competitive instincts, sharpening my
knife and my skills while plotting my rise to the head table, only to
learn the seating arrangement is up to the Master in charge. Yahweh
Sisters, we can preen, claw, and jockey our way toward the top, but
we may never make it. Worse, we may make it and find it unsuit-
able or unsatisfying. Better that we hold our power under restraint,
remain focused on Christ, and be ushered to the front table at His
calling.

Let's opt for the freedom that comes with killing our competitive urges, and let God exalt us to the seats He has saved for us.
Meanwhile, we can use all that extra time and energy to serve others.

BIBLE STUDY

1. How's your God-sight been lately? When our hearts lack
   humility—when they are tainted with a selfish desire to be
   exalted—our ability to see beyond ourselves dwindles. Read
   Matthew 5:8, and write down what it takes to see God.

2. We're blessed by God when we serve contentedly rather than grasp to satisfy our pride or advance ourselves. Look up these Old Testament verses and record their teaching on pride and humility:

Proverbs 8:12–13

Proverbs 16:5

Proverbs 16:9

Proverbs 16:18

Proverbs 16:19

Proverbs 25:6–7

Proverbs 29:23

3. In the final weeks before Jesus' crucifixion, He traveled between towns with His disciples before heading into Jerusalem. He knew what awaited Him there, and that His time with the Twelve was limited. Read these four scenes from that time period.

Mark 8:34–35

Mark 9:33–35

Mark 10:29–31

Mark 10:42–45

What point does Jesus drive home in each of these discussions with His followers?

4. Philippians 2 brings me to my knees, which is unexpected given that the letter is basically a thank-you note from Paul to

the Christians in Philippi who'd sent him a gift. Apparently Paul wanted to bless them in return—by reminding them of the power of downward mobility. Read Philippians 2:1–11. Underline parts that stand out to you.

5. Jesus frequently took the religious leaders to task for prideful motives and actions. Read Matthew 23:1–12. List five things Jesus calls them on in this passage. Then write your own motto based on Jesus' final statement in verse 12.

4

Keep a Heavenly Lawyer on Retainer

Revealing the Secret to Handling Conflicts Biblically

I'm a word girl, not a math girl. Fractions, equations, and I don't jive. However, in sixth grade I scored high on my end-of-grade math test. I have no idea how, other than I must've eaten Wheaties that morning. Convinced it was indicative of gifted math abilities, the school skipped me ahead, putting me in eighth-grade algebra as a seventh-grader.

I still recall the potent mixture of humiliation and anger I felt one day in that algebra class when I sat down and saw a horrible message scribbled on my desk. Searching my backpack for an eraser, I flushed with embarrassment. It was sixth period, which means five other math classes might have already seen it—five other *eighth-grade classes* no less. The desk read: "Rachel is a big fat cow."

Mortified, I fought back tears for the next fifteen minutes while struggling to understand the lecture on square roots.

A handful of years prior, I'd skipped across the playground singing, "Sticks and stones can break my bones, but words can never hurt me." What a lie that little ditty is.

> "You're familiar with the command to the ancients, 'Do not murder.' I'm telling you that anyone who is so much as angry with a brother or sister is guilty of murder. Carelessly call a brother 'idiot!' and you just might find yourself hauled into court. Thoughtlessly yell 'stupid!' at a sister and you are on the brink of hellfire. The simple moral fact is that words kill." (Matt. 5:21–22 MSG)

While sticks and stones break bones, words warp minds. They wound souls. They can shatter one's entire concept of self, God, or others. And a negative critique of a young girl's figure? That can cause nuclear fallout.

I was not overweight. In fact, as a competitive gymnast training more than ten hours a week, I was extremely fit. However, I was bigger than most girls my age. Training built my calves, chiseled my thighs, and defined my biceps. Adding to the muscles were curves. I had rounded out hips and a chest earlier than most—which made staying on the balance beam even trickier. By seventh grade I was wearing a size 9 while my peers were still in 3s and 5s.

Right away I was sure who had written the insult: Jolene. I've changed her name to protect her identity. I chose this pseudonym because she also stole my boyfriend one summer while I was on vacation. Dolly Parton's song "Jolene" serves as the soundtrack for that memory. Sorry, but I'm southern and love me some Dolly.

Staring at the put-down in her telltale handwriting, I wanted to hurt Jolene the way this hurt me. *Who does she think she is?* I wanted her to drop off the face of the earth. *She's about my size—we could probably share clothes. That makes her a fat cow too!* Jolene was athletic as well.

> "Don't pick on people, jump on their failures, criticize their faults—unless, of course, you want the same treatment. That critical spirit has a way of boomeranging." (Matt. 7:1–2 MSG)

Frenemies

In theory Jolene and I were friends. We ran with the same crowd. We lived in the same neighborhood. And we were on the same athletic squad. We had quite a bit in common.

Behind the scenes, however, I felt she was out to get me. Sometimes subtly, other times—like the desk incident—more blatantly. Once at a middle school gymnastic competition she sat in the bleachers by the bars loudly chanting, "Fall! Fall! Fall!" while I performed for the judges. Later she claimed to be kidding.

That's a memory I can't forget—it's captured in a photo in my yearbook. There she sits in the stands and there I am, mid-hip to the high bar, with underarm sweat spots visible on my leotard. Lovely. I'm not sure if I was sweating from the exertion of competition or from that familiar mix of humiliation and pain Jolene so easily evoked.

Ever had a "frenemy" like Jolene? It messes with your head and your heart. I found myself alternately crying and seething, fighting back, and trying to convince myself I didn't care. And every once in a while, I wished we could just be friends.

Her animosity and veiled insults continued through high school. I was relieved to leave for college and get Jolene out of my hair. Yet then I discovered there were plenty of other "Jolenes" to contend with in the dorm, in the workplace, in the neighborhood, and sometimes even in the church.

Mind-Game Show

What's a gal to do when she's on the losing end of a mind-game with a Jolene? Must she be a good sport about it? How does she cope? Can anything good come out of these situations? Can't she at least get a consolation prize for being in the game?

On the TV game show *Let's Make a Deal,* prizes lay hidden behind three different doors. The contestant had to choose one door. It might reveal a sports car or a can of Spam—players desperately wanted to choose the most beneficial door. When we're emotionally hurting at the hands of someone else, we have three options to choose from as well.

Door Number One

We can try numbing our hearts with things like food, shopping, dieting, decorating, or frozen margaritas. I know from experience that this works—temporarily—only to then add additional troubles to your life. It's a false solution that compounds rather than solves problems. Nonetheless, we choose the numbing option often because it's a quick, easy fix offering immediate—though not lasting—relief.

Have you noticed avoiding pain is a top priority for people? Saint Augustine, living 1600 years ago, did. He said, "All sin is committed by our desire for a good life and our fear of pain. But the things we do for a good life are lies that make us even more miserable than before." Smart dude.

Door Number Two

The next option is twisting the pain into anger and going on the offensive. Anger is no picnic, but it seems easier to digest than pain. Attacking feels more productive than aching, obsessing, or numbing. We can outwit our enemy. Top her. Exact our revenge. And maybe, just maybe, manage to restore our self-esteem in the process.

What a deceptive notion, that we can heal our own souls. What an alluring thought, that we can rebuild ourselves by tearing others down.

Revenge makes a terrible companion. She mooches our time and energy, rarely making good on her promises. The Bible says, "See that no one pays back evil for evil, but always try to do good to each other and to everyone else" (1 Thess. 5:15).

Door Number Three

So our final option is to drop the spoon or the stone we're clenching and actually feel the pain we're in. This seems the scariest possible choice.

When we're injured, we hurt. There's no denying that. There's no avoiding it. The trick is to acknowledge the pain we feel and turn it over to Christ. In feeling the pain of an insult or offense and not returning the slight, we share in the suffering of Christ: "This suffering is all part of what God has called you to. Christ, who suffered for you, is your example. Follow in his steps" (1 Peter 2:21).

This last option is not for the faint of heart, it is for the faithful of heart. Not fighting back is hard to do, but I've come to regard it as a worthwhile, even exciting challenge. (More on that in a minute.) To do this, you'll have to stomach the uncomfortable feeling of powerlessness until your faith takes hold of the truth that as a Yahweh Sister, following in His steps is by far your smartest move.

If You Can't Say Anything Nice …

Handing our pain and thirst for revenge over to Christ is not only our smartest move, it's our only legitimate move when we're living for God's kingdom. The empire may strike back, but that's not what we are called to do.

Paul explains:

> Never pay back evil for evil to anyone. Do things in such a way that everyone can see you are honorable. Do your part to live in peace with everyone, as much as possible. Dear friends, never avenge yourselves. Leave that to God. For it is written, "I will take vengeance; I will repay those who deserve it," says the Lord. Instead, do what the Scriptures say: "If your enemies are hungry, feed them. If they are thirsty, give them something to drink, and they will be ashamed of what they have done to you."

> Don't let evil get the best of you, but conquer evil
> by doing good. (Rom. 12:17–21)

Paul refers to a statement Yahweh made in Deuteronomy 32:35 declaring that vengeance belongs to Him. Revenge is not our prerogative. Judging people and distributing justice is God's jurisdiction.

We can trust Yahweh to judge fairly and to repay when necessary. That's super important to note. Have you ever retaliated with words or actions when you felt wronged, only to learn you had misunderstood the situation? Open mouth; insert foot.

Ever planned your revenge and carried it out, only to find it didn't work or wasn't as sweet as anticipated? Deflating. Ever waited for a chance to get even and never got the opportunity? Frustrating. Ever demanded an apology only to receive silence or further insult? Maddening! When we trust God with the situation, He gets at the core of the matter, enacting perfect justice. Evil is punished, persecutors are penalized, and we experience peace.

Realize, however, it may take longer than you imagine. Yahweh does this in His timing. Proverbs 20:22 advises, "Do not say, 'I'll pay you back for this wrong!' Wait for the LORD, and he will deliver you" (NIV).

Trusting the One Who Justifies

Waiting on God is rarely easy, but always worth it. King David knew this. After all, he'd always found God to be trustworthy.

A member of David's family made a play to take the throne from him forcefully, so the king and his men left Jerusalem, traveling past the town of Bahurim. There, a man named Shimei came out of the village, cursing and pelting them with rocks.

"Get out of here, you murderer, you scoundrel!" Shimei shouted at David (2 Sam. 16:7). He claimed David killed his predecessor, King Saul, in a bloodthirsty quest to steal the throne for himself. It simply wasn't true.

God had chosen David as king, and it was Saul who tried to kill David. The young king actually spared Saul's life more than once. Good thing God is our sole Judge and not others who do not know or understand the truth.

"Why should this dead dog curse my lord the king? ... Let me go over and cut off his head!" David's servant Abishai demanded after Shimei's verbal tirade (v. 9). Our friends, in a misguided attempt to show their loyalty, can tempt us into retaliating. David, however, prevented Abishai from harming Shimei.

King David instructed his soldiers to let the angry man curse him. Can you imagine? Then the king added, "And perhaps the LORD will see that I am being wronged and will bless me because of these curses" (v. 12). Ah, so there's a reason David let Shimei continue with the cursing—and it wasn't low self-esteem. He knew returning cursing with blessing pleases God. David and his men journeyed on, with Shimei following along on the ridge of the hill, kicking up dust, cursing, and throwing stones at them as they went.

A good while later, after the people of Jerusalem called their exiled king to return to his home and throne, David and Shimei met up again. This time along the banks of the Jordan River, where Shimei behaved quite differently:

> Shimei son of Gera bowed deeply in homage to the
> king as soon as he was across the Jordan and said,

"Don't think badly of me, my master! Overlook my irresponsible outburst on the day my master the king left Jerusalem—don't hold it against me! I know I sinned, but look at me now—the first of all the tribe of Joseph to come down and welcome back my master the king!"

Abishai son of Zeruiah interrupted, "Enough of this! Shouldn't we kill him outright? Why, he cursed GOD's anointed!"

But David said, "What is it with you sons of Zeruiah? Why do you insist on being so contentious? Nobody is going to be killed today. I am again king over Israel!"

Then the king turned to Shimei, "You're not going to die." And the king gave him his word. (2 Samuel 19:18–23 MSG)

Just as David had spared Saul's life twice, he spared Shimei's twice—even though both men were his sworn enemies. Why? Because David trusted God to defend him when slighted, and to justify him when wronged—even if it took some time. Living for God's kingdom requires trust, patience, and long-range thinking.

Entering Your Plea

We've all been slighted at some point. A coworker steals your idea and takes it to the boss as her own. A friend drops you when you're walking through the valley of job loss and can't afford to shop and play as before. Your Bible study partner promises not tell anyone your problem, but then calls forty of her closest friends. Jolene moves in on your man.

Usually when I feel slighted or offended, it's not that I want to exact revenge. I'm much too nonconfrontational to carry out vengeful schemes. Oh, I've dreamt up some doozies, but I don't have the chutzpa to enact them. I don't want people to think badly of me, so I try not to act like Shimei.

What I typically want most is to defend myself in these situations. I want to enter my not-guilty plea and argue my case. I want my day in court. I want the record set straight, and I want veneration so I can protect my reputation.

I don't wish to remain silent like David. I don't wish to stop my friends from evening the score. If I can't defend myself, I want someone to do it for me.

Can I get a court-appointed lawyer?

Persecuted, Job wanted such a lawyer as well. His friends accused him of being so sinful that he caused God to punish him severely. Job cried out: "O Earth, don't cover up the wrong done to me! Don't muffle my cry! There must be Someone in heaven who knows the truth about me, in highest heaven, some Attorney who can clear my name—my Champion, my Friend, while I'm weeping my eyes out before God. I appeal to the One who represents mortals before God as a neighbor stands up for a neighbor" (Job 16:18–20 MSG). A great many years before Mary gave birth to Christ, Job was calling on Him in heaven for defense.

According to God, we have a heavenly court-appointed lawyer: Jesus. Furthermore, He is the best possible lawyer for He was there when the Law was written. And He never loses a case—"The LORD says to Jerusalem: 'I will be your lawyer to plead your case, and I will avenge you'" (Jer. 51:36). Yahweh Sisters, keep a heavenly lawyer on retainer!

This lawyer never misses a day in court. The author of Hebrews writes, "Jesus remains a priest forever; his priesthood will never end. Therefore he is able, once and forever, to save everyone who comes to God through him. He lives forever to plead with God on their behalf" (Heb. 7:24–25). Christ is constantly available, working pro bono to defend those who come to Him.

Christ the lawyer can empathize with His clients—knowing how it feels to be wronged, hurt, and falsely accused. He understands our plight. He's been there. He was doubted, hunted, betrayed, spit at, beaten, mocked, insulted, and reviled—and "he did not retaliate when he was insulted. When he suffered, he did not threaten to get even. He left his case in the hands of God, who always judges fairly" (1 Peter 2:23). He was also wrongfully killed on a cross, thereby passing the heavenly bar to become our appointed lawyer.

He Said, She Said

Let me tell you about the time I learned to rely on His legal counsel. I found myself in a spat with a Yahweh Sister with whom I served on a committee. She held a position on the steering team for this committee. Though I did not serve in leadership, I was an active member. When the time came to appoint a new steering chairwoman, another leader suggested I throw my hat in the ring. After praying about it, I did—only to find my friend extremely upset with me.

She felt that job was due her since she had been serving on the leadership team and I had not. Furthermore, she took it as a personal offense that I, her friend, would put myself in the running for it. Truth is, I didn't expect her to want the job. She was convinced, however, that I was consciously usurping her, and she told others as much.

It grieved my heart. Not only because I felt unfairly portrayed to others, but also because our friendship hung in the balance. I cried and prayed for two days over this.

Then God's Word challenged my spirit not to say a single word in attack or defense. I sensed I should lay down the committee position, and value the relationship above all else. My goal became to trust Christ as my heavenly lawyer and let Him exonerate me, or humble me, as He saw fit. I was willing to accept either outcome.

Reaching this place of forgiveness and resolve to let God defend me didn't come easily or naturally. Once I reached it, however, I actually found myself excited! I wasn't sure what, if anything, would come of it, but it felt empowering to trust God so completely. He laid down His life for me, surely I could lay down this role or my reputation to follow and reflect Him.

I told the committee—without making any arguments in my defense or in her prosecution—that I was withdrawing my name from consideration. Then I called my friend to say I could see where she was coming from, and that I was sorry I had hurt her feelings. I told her that was never my intention, and that I'd withdrawn from the race.

Let's clarify something. From a young age I perfected the art of the non-apologizing apology. If you've mastered this too, you know exactly what I'm talking about. You can apologize, particularly when forced to, and not really admit to any wrongdoing. You can say you're sorry, and sound it but not mean it. But this is not what I was doing.

She rattled on in angry frustration, making her case against me. I expected as much and simply listened. Occasionally I would "uh-huh" in acknowledgment or respond, "I'm sorry you feel like this. I hope our friendship can remain intact."

Our mostly one-way conversation lasted nearly an hour. Multiple times I bit my lip and prayed under my breath in order to remain silent (I'm a communication major who loved debate class, after all). Each time I yielded the stand to my heavenly lawyer, I grew stronger in my resolve to trust God with this. I also grew more gracious in my feelings and response toward my friend. That's what you call walking by the Spirit and not the flesh.

The Verdict Is …

To my amazement, by the end of the conversation she was insisting I put my name back in the running for consideration. As she talked on and I remained quiet or gracious, she arrived at the conclusion that I was the best person for the job. In fact, she made the call to reenter my name. I was appointed the leadership role, and we worked happily side by side. That was many years ago, but I still run into her occasionally, and we are friends to this day. All because I bit my tongue in favor of letting Christ argue my case.

Rather than seeking vengeance or gunning for veneration as I typically would, I sought God and asked for His perspective. I learned to pray, "Not my will but Yours be done" before taking aim or taking action—and to mean it. (Sometimes I have to keep praying it until I can mean it.)

This incident was truly transforming for me. Having experienced this, I no longer wish to be a vigilante, settling my own accounts and doling out punishment as I see fit. Now, I place a prayer call to my heavenly lawyer and trust Him as my representation and judge. Things work out … so much better.

When to Put Down Your Dukes

Please note, Yahweh Sisters, I'm not suggesting silent endurance of domestic violence, or sexual abuse, or compliance with an employer engaging in something unethical. I'm talking about "turning the other cheek" at those interpersonal slights that cause us to get our britches in a wad. (I've never actually seen britches wad but, according to my nana, it happens.) What I'm suggesting, just as the Bible does, is that we not be so easily offended. And when we are hurt, to take it to Jesus rather than taking it out on others.

"Don't get mad, get even!" is the world's response to mistreatment. "Don't tread on me" is the motto. "We're not gonna take it," we sing. That's because it goes against our every natural impulse to watch our enemy get off seemingly scot-free.

The secret truth is, when we leave justice in God's capable hands, He promises He will defend and vindicate. He even blesses us for showing obedient endurance and trust. We can rest confidently in that truth, knowing we're also growing in godly character, reflecting Christ's uncommon image.

Being insulted, mistreated, or persecuted—especially for our faith—isn't cause for numbing, anger, or retaliation. Rather it's cause for prayerful rejoicing over the opportunity to demonstrate (or increase) the extent of our trust in God.

In God's kingdom, painful situations are catalysts for glorious transformation. When we turn to Him in these matters, our wounds are dressed, our souls healed, and we glimpse Him lovingly at work on our behalf. We're also delivered from the agony of resentment or the regret of misguided revenge.

One Last Tear

While helping out in my dad's restaurant one Saturday a few years after high school, I spotted Jolene. Our eyes met, my adrenaline surged, and I tried to pretend I didn't recognize her. It didn't work. She was making a beeline for me.

In the years since I'd last seen Jolene, I'd found Jesus. I'd learned His ways of living and become more secure in the core of myself. Yet at that moment, I felt familiar feelings of panic, persecution, and pain. Old patterns sometimes die hard. As she moved closer, I clinched my sweaty palms and braced myself for the impact of her words.

She beamed a smile, said hello, and asked me how I was doing. I gave one-word answers. She kept talking, drawing me into conversation. I was suspicious, hesitant.

We traded updates on mutual friends. She was pleasant. Eventually I relaxed and even enjoyed our brief chat.

"Well, I'd better get back over to my group," she said, nodding toward her friends.

"Yeah, I've got to get back to work," I said.

"It's been nice talking to you."

"Yeah, you too."

Jolene walked about two yards before spinning around sharply.

It caught my breath. With surprising sincerity she said, "I don't know why we weren't better friends in high school."

My jaw dropped, stunned. I pulled it up quickly and managed a smile. She smiled back sweetly, spun on her heels, and headed back to her friends.

Once in the safe cocoon of the kitchen, with commercial dish-washers abuzz around me, I paced the floor. My mind whirled with confusing thoughts, like a mix of dirty-clean dishwater:

So that's it? That's what years of being public frenemy number one amounts to? A three-minute conversation where you act like circumstances beyond your control kept us from being friends? What do you mean you don't know why we weren't better friends?! Because you hated me! Because you insulted me! Because you tormented me!

Maybe it was the soothing sound of water rushing through the machines, reminding me that Jesus washes all things clean, but my indignant rage subsided. A single tear of relief streaked through my blush. *I don't know why we couldn't be friends either, Jolene.*

I thought of all the Jolene-wasted years and tears. How different things might have been had she or I brought Jesus on the scene long ago. It was a massive realization and a memorable lesson. By the time I emerged from the kitchen, her party had left.

That night, nestled beneath my cotton covers, I reflected on my reunion with Jolene. Drifting off, I dreamed of a world where Jolene and I were great friends. There were no jabs, no insults, and no tears. Loving-kindness dominated our every interaction. I think it was heaven, and I fully believe it exists.

And if you need the name of a good lawyer there, I have one.

BIBLE STUDY

1. The account of Moses and Pharaoh in Exodus 1—15 is a dramatic story about God's deliverance and His vengeance on those who mistreat His people.

   Read Exodus 5:22—6:5. Moses grew impatient with God allowing His people to suffer awhile before punishing their abusers. Yet Yahweh doesn't seem too worried about that! Now read Exodus 6:6–8, 7:3–5, 9:13–18, and 14:1–4.

   Who is calling the shots here, and who only thinks they are?

   What is God's underlying purpose, revealed in these passages?

   Are you OK with suffering awhile for that purpose?

   Imagine you are with the Hebrew people there in chapter 14, stuck between the approaching Egyptians and the Red

Sea. God has just delivered you from slavery in Egypt, but now it seems you're caught again. Seeing nowhere to run, you have to choose door number three and trust God.

The people didn't like being in this position—they needed greater faith in God's ability and willingness to save. Read Exodus 14:10–14. Write the instructions and promises given to them just before the sea miraculously parted.

2. We've been talking about letting God defend us when we're wrongfully treated or falsely accused. But Jesus is every bit our defense lawyer when we sin, shielding us from the punishment we rightfully deserve. To see your attorney in action, read John 8:1–11.

What do you imagine Jesus wrote?

Why do you think the oldest were the first to drop their rocks and walk?

3. Perhaps you are wondering if there are ever instances when it's OK to confront someone who has sinned or wronged you. Yes, there are—see Luke 17:3, 2 Thessalonians 3:15, and Matthew 18:15–17. Write down how to go about this—it's not with guns or tongues a'blazing!

4. Religious leaders in Jesus' day taught you must forgive someone who wrongs you up to three times. But if they did it a fourth time, all bets were off! Peter suspects Jesus will ask him to be more forgiving than that and asks Him about it. Read their discussion in Matthew 18:21–35.

How many times should you forgive someone? What do you think this means?

At what point are you free to retaliate?

5. We have to put to death our inner Judge Judy. We're just not cut out to be judge and jury of our own cases. So let's take off the black robes, lay down our briefcase of facts, and

allow God to go to work. Proverbs 30:5 assures us, "Every word of God proves true. He defends all who come to him for protection." There is something satisfying about submitting ourselves to God and being content with His dealings with us. Is there a case you need to discuss with Him today? Explain.

5

Have Eyes Bigger Than your Stomach

Revealing the Secret of Living Generously

Chilled air entwines my wrists as I maneuver the tongs. I'm facing one of my ongoing dilemmas: how to make a reasonable-sized salad on my plate. Somehow, a well-stocked salad bar causes me to lose all sense of spatial perception. No matter how hard I try, I just can't make a small salad.

When I took more food than I could eat as a young girl, my grandmother would quip, "Rachel, your eyes are bigger than your stomach!" She didn't bother to explain her sayings, and they didn't always make sense in my mind. *How can two eyes be bigger than a whole stomach?*

Nana hid other gems of wisdom in bizarre wording. Like this one she declared to me with some frequency: "Green-eyed greedy gut, run around, eat the world up!" *Why is she telling me a monster story? Is this about me? I thought my eyes were brown.* Frankly, I wondered about her sanity. Now, however, it makes perfect sense. She was pointing out my unchecked desire to take, have, and hoard for myself.

Give this Way

Jesus understands my greedy-gut ways. And He knows that even when people are generous—when we do give—half the time we're hoping for some recognition in return. A thank-you card, a plaque, an atta-girl, an IOU, *something*. He talked about it in the Sermon on the Mount. Let's take some time to look at that passage together.

Matthew 6 begins with twenty verses of Jesus instructing His listeners to give, pray, and fast without drawing attention to themselves. While many give desiring publicity, Jesus just isn't a fan of the big-check-photo-op style of giving. He values secret giving. See what I mean in verses 1–4:

> Take care! Don't do your good deeds publicly, to be admired, because then you will lose the reward from your Father in heaven. When you give a gift to someone in need, don't shout about it as the hypocrites do—blowing trumpets in the synagogues and streets to call attention to their acts of charity! I assure you, they have received all the reward they will ever get. But when you give to someone, don't tell your left hand what your right hand is doing. Give your gifts in secret, and your Father, who knows all secrets, will reward you.

Jesus isn't just correcting our motives here, He is also assuring us that when we give without making a big deal of it, we can trust that God sees and will reward us. Don't miss that promise ... or its prerequisite.

The thing that jumps out at me in this passage is that Jesus *assumes* His followers give. Not just to the church offering plate or building fund, not just to the mail carrier at Christmas time, but to people around us in need. Jesus said, "*When* you give a gift to someone in need ..." Pause and ask yourself, *Do I wake even most mornings with the assumption that I will give to someone in need today?*

Banking on It

Continuing in Jesus' famous sermon we find sound financial planning tips within a few verses. Matthew 6:19–21:

> Don't store up treasures here on earth, where they can be eaten by moths and get rusty, and where thieves break in and steal. Store your treasures in heaven, where they will never become moth-eaten or rusty and where they will be safe from thieves. Wherever your treasure is, there your heart and thoughts will also be.

Jesus is revealing another kingdom secret: We have a divine savings plan! While on earth, we can make deposits into heaven. I picture the "Alpha and Omega Savings and Loan." It is fail-proof, fireproof, and theft-proof. Plus, it offers an astonishing rate of return on our deposits—as much as one-thousand-fold!

I pay into social security and a 401(k) retirement account to prepare for the later years of my life on earth, but Jesus is instructing me to prepare for eternity by storing up treasure in heaven.

Wondering how to do that? Thought you might be. Hold that thought; we'll get there.

At the end of these verses about laying up treasure in heaven, Jesus tells us that our hearts, thoughts, and treasure are all interconnected. They're interdependent. Intertwined. Why does He point this out? Because if I need help with my hoarding tendency, I can focus my thoughts on heaven.

Looking beyond today into eternity, I find a bigger salad or a larger closet is not what my soul truly needs or craves. I discover my future lies not on Wall Street, the Sunset Strip, or Madison Avenue, but on Yahweh's streets of gold. C. S. Lewis said, "If I find in myself a desire which no experience in this world can satisfy, the most probable explanation is that I was made for another world."[1] Yahweh Sisters are indeed made for another world.

Eyes, Lamps, and Masters

Continuing in Matthew 6 we arrive at verses 22–24. Take a look:

> Your eye is a lamp for your body. A pure eye lets
> sunshine into your soul. But an evil eye shuts out
> the light and plunges you into darkness. If the light
> you think you have is really darkness, how deep
> that darkness will be!

> No one can serve two masters. For you will hate
> one and love the other, or be devoted to one and
> despise the other. You cannot serve both God and
> money.

I easily track with Jesus in verses 1–21: Give, pray, fast—and don't do these spiritual things expecting an earthly reward from people. Then God will reward you in heavenly ways. Got it.

Confusion used to set in, however, around verse 22 where Jesus mentions pure and evil eyes. I thought the evil eye was that look your friend shoots you when you're about to reveal her age. Or, that look your husband shoots you when you tell your mother, "We'd love you to stay another night!" Not understanding these eye verses, I glossed past them when reading.

I understood Jesus' point that we cannot serve two masters well. He makes clear that a divided heart is not productive. And He spells out the specific two masters He's talking about: God and money. Here is our warning that if we build our life around obtaining or spending money, it will affect our heart and thoughts in ways that push out God.

I don't want money squeezing God from my mind, but if I shun money, how will I pay for my car, or my jeans, or my anti-cellulite cream? We have little choice but to interact with money. We must earn, save, and spend because that's how our world operates.

Money itself isn't evil, rather the *love* of money (Heb. 13:5). I don't believe Jesus is instructing us to shun bills and coins in favor of bartering. Rather, we must manage our money in such a way that deposits treasure in heaven and keeps us connected with God while on earth.

So how do we do that? The key, I discovered, is in the eye verses I ignored when I didn't understand them. I learned the phrase *pure eye* in this verse is an idiom in the Hebrew language meaning "generous." A pure eye is an eye that sees the needs of others and is willing to meet them. Likewise, an "evil eye" is a Hebrew idiom meaning "selfishness." An evil eye is an eye that ignores the needs of others in favor of taking, having, and holding for oneself. It's the green-eyed greedy gut who runs around eating the world up.

Jesus teaches in this sermon that we'll keep open to God, store up treasure in heaven, and prosper eternally by living generously on earth. However, when we're covetous, greedy, and selfish, we push God from our hearts and minds and wind up with money as our master. We'll have little eternal reward to show for that.

In 1 Timothy 6:17–19 (NIV) Paul further explains how to deposit treasure in heaven:

> Command those who are rich in this present world not to be arrogant nor to put their hope in wealth, which is so uncertain, but to put their hope in God, who richly provides us with everything for our enjoyment. Command them to do good, to be rich in good deeds, and to be generous and willing to share. In this way they will lay up treasure for themselves as a firm foundation for the coming age, so that they may take hold of the life that is truly life.

Who Is Rich?

You may be wondering if Paul was talking about you with his instructions to the "rich in this present world." I did. My home is of modest size, nearly a thousand square feet smaller than the American average. I'm currently driving an eight-year-old vehicle. I typically buy on sale to stay on budget. Do I qualify as the rich in this world? Do you?

Chances are, if you had the money to buy this book or the car to drive to the library and borrow it, you are. Chances are, if you have the discretionary time to read books as well as the education to comprehend words like *comprehend,* you are. Compared to most of the world, you and I are wealthy. So let me ask, are we also generous? Are we transferring any of that wealth to heaven by giving to help others?

Looking back at verse 23 in Matthew 6, Jesus warned, "If the light you think you have is really darkness, how deep that darkness will be!" In other words, a self-deceived person is likely to stay that way. It's possible to think we're generous when in reality we are selfish and self-deceived. German poet Johann Wolfgang von Goethe advised, "Don't say that you want to give, but go ahead and give! You'll never catch up with a mere hope."

Perhaps you are not rich by the world's standards. Maybe you don't own a home or a car. And maybe you wish I'd stop using big five-dollar words. Does that let you off the giving hook?

Ask the disciples who lived hand-to-mouth as they followed Jesus.

Ask the widow who gave just two small coins. Jesus praised her above all the big givers, knowing hers was the largest sacrifice.

If we're not compelled to live generously, it's because we've got an "eye problem," a vision problem. We've lost sight of who God is and what He does. We've forgotten the mercy of His salvation, the grace of His presence, not to mention the blessing of His divine savings plan. If we aren't interested in depositing treasure in heaven, we've lost sight of the fact that this world—and all its treats and treasure—is temporary. We've developed a nasty case of evil eye.

Oh, that Jesus would open our eyes to this truth! Oh, that He would help us unfurl our fists, and begin living openhandedly—trusting God to provide both for and through us.

When You Care Enough

I still remember receiving Aunt Susie's cards every birthday and Christmas. My parents owned a chain of Hallmark stores, so I'd seen a lot of cards. Hers were never fancy, and to my recollection, never from Hallmark. But she definitely cared enough to send the very best. Each card was stuffed with a five-dollar bill and signed the same way: *With love, Aunt Susie R. Madigan.*

My great-aunt was one of my favorite people ever to have walked the earth. No one would consider her beautiful or line up to be her date. She had minimal education from a country school. Upward mobility is something she knew nothing about. She never owned a car or even learned to drive. She wasn't articulate or dynamic and possessed no special skills, beyond gracious kindness. But to me she was love … living, walking, breathing, selfless love.

My babysitter of choice, Aunt Susie told me stories for hours on end, tirelessly repeating my favorites. I rarely watched TV when Susie was around. Knowing I liked peas, she'd fish all the peas out of her bowl of vegetable soup and put them in mine. When I was sick, she'd rub my forehead for hours.

Susie also took care of her neighbors when they grew ill or senile. She even chose a second floor, two-room apartment overlooking a funeral home so she could pray for the families coming through there in their time of grief. I'm convinced many people benefited from her prayers, people who never knew her.

Widowed early, with no children, Aunt Susie went from blue collar to almost collarless. Yet she loved, gave, prayed, and served selflessly and happily. She is the picture in my head of living generously. She's passed away now, but I'm certain her present life with Christ is rich.

Scraping By

Imagine for a minute you are a poor widow living several hundred years before Christ. You've lost your husband, which in your era means you've lost pretty much everything. You have no status in the community and no income. There's no unemployment commission or welfare system. No social security checks either. You have a young son, and your heart breaks because you can no longer support him.

You've tried all you know to try. You've sold all you have to sell. And to make matters worse, the whole land is in a severe drought, and food is scare.

You get up one morning; it's the beginning of the end. All your food jars are scraping bottom. After today's one small meal, there'll be no more to eat. You've known this day was coming. You've stressed about it, prayed about it, and tried to make peace with its dire reality.

As you head out to gather sticks to build a fire, your stomach growls. Used to the sound, you focus on scouring the edge of town for dry wood and anything edible you can find.

There you encounter a man who asks you to give him food and water. Food is in short supply, and this man is asking you, a widow, to give him bread? You kindly reply that you have only a little bit left, and once you fix it today for you and your son, you will begin to starve. Undeterred, he again requests you give him some food and promises that after you do, there will still be more in the jar to feed you and your son.

Whaaat? This is crazy! His request goes against every self-protective instinct you have. It violates every mothering instinct you have, which would have you kill a bear with your bare hands if it were the only way to get your child some food. But there are no bears around these parts—and there's no food either. And he wants you to give away your last morsel?

Yet he is a man of God, promising if you do this, God Himself will ensure you have enough food to last until the drought ends. Wouldn't that be wonderful! But how? Could this be for real? You have to give away the last bite of life-sustaining food to find out.

Though I grew up with a great example of a gracious, giving woman in my life, I've struggled to be that way myself. I tend to be selfish and self-protective—only wanting to give after I'm sure I've got enough for me and mine. I want to give once I have a surplus to give out of. God says, "Give in faith, and then I'll provide the surplus" (Luke 6:38, author's paraphrase).

There is a certain woman in the Old Testament—a widow from the village of Zarephath—who lived this exact experience. She took the risk. She gave. She gave not out of her surplus, but out of her destitution.

She gave the last of her food to the prophet Elijah and found, miraculously, there was yet more. For days on end, each time she reached into her flour and oil jars to make food, there was just enough for Elijah, herself, and her son (check out her story in 1 Kings 17:7–24). God provided through and for her.

My Yahweh Sister, when is the last time you took a leap of trust, a leap of faith, to give? I don't mean buying Christmas presents on credit, trusting you'll be able to pay that off come January! I mean you followed what you felt God nudging you to do and gave, even though it didn't necessarily make sense to you.

Making a Deposit

It was the Thursday after the economic crash of 2008, the Thursday after the 700-billion-dollar bank bailout package passed Congress. On this Thursday, gas prices sat at four dollars per gallon, the Dow sat about four hundred points down, and Americans sat wondering if they would lose their jobs in the coming months. Many did. America teetered on the edge of economic drought.

Having a bank debit card, I don't keep much cash in my wallet. In fact, it had been a couple weeks since I'd had any cash at all. So when I stopped at the bank to deposit my paycheck, I got twenty-five dollars.

Driving home down a busy street, I noticed a man in the distance standing in the median between double sets of lanes. He was waiting for a break in traffic to walk across. Almost immediately the thought popped in my head, "*Give him money.*"

My first reaction was to rationalize. *He might be dangerous. He might use it to buy street drugs.* My second reaction was to condemn the thought. *Rachel, just because someone is walking instead of driving doesn't mean they don't have enough money. Gosh, how shallow of me to assume that. He might be insulted if I offered him money.*

As I drove closer, I saw he was wearing a reddish short-sleeve shirt with a collar and faded black pants. *Maybe he is crossing over to work at that Burger King, or that Kmart—see, he probably has money.* But again I felt the urge to give to him. *Why? How?* I was traveling at forty miles per hour in traffic. Doubt swirled through my head as my car sailed right past him.

As I passed by, I sensed I was passing up an opportunity from God. I decided if this was God speaking to me, I didn't want to miss it. And if it wasn't God, the worst-case scenario is I'm out a few bucks. After weighing these two possibilities on the scale of my mind, I turned the car around at the next intersection and picked up my wallet. I had a twenty- and a five-dollar bill. I pulled out the twenty.

Now my car was traveling in the direction he was facing. *How will I slow down enough to give it to him without causing an accident?* The traffic parted as I got into the far lane on his side. I looked in my rearview mirror, surprised to see no other cars behind me for a long distance. I slowed to a stop, lowered the window, and thrust out my hand with the money. Not knowing what else to say (he hadn't been begging) I announced, "God bless."

Without hesitating, he smiled brightly, took it, and simply said, "Thank you." He seemed humbly thankful, but not very surprised. It was almost like he expected it—like maybe he'd prayed for it. I matched his grin and then hit the gas pedal again.

What does it matter if he needed the money or not? What's it to me how he spends it? As far as it concerned me, it only mattered that I obeyed God when I felt He was directing me to give.

Do You Want Cash Back?

It would be neat if I could report God rewarded me by placing a hundred-dollar bill in my path later that day. Sometimes God does that sort of *"See—you can trust Me!"* thing. But I think I'm just going to have to wait for a divine dividend on this one. And I'm cool with that. Some might say I'm sacrificing any reward by sharing this story. I'm cool with that, too—which is major progress for a green-eyed greedy gut. But I don't think so, because God always judges based on motive. My motive for giving that day was to obey God, not to be noticed by others and given a spiritual merit badge.

I believe someday—maybe here or maybe in eternity—I'll see evidence that giving the twenty dollars was the same as depositing it. Anne Frank said, "No one has ever become poor by giving." This is a lesson I've had to learn over and over because I slip all too easily into my greedy-gut ways. My willingness to give my own money has waxed and waned like the phases of the moon. But it's the moments that I've chosen to give that I remember, and Jesus assures that Yahweh will remember as well.

Randy Alcorn writes in *Money, Possessions, and Eternity*: "God keeps an account open for us in heaven, and every gift given for His glory is a deposit in that account. Not only God, not only others, but we are the eternal beneficiaries of our giving."[2] I receive statements from the government and my 401(k) account showing me how much money I've accrued for retirement so far. Can you imagine if we got statements from "Alpha and Omega Savings and Loan"? What would your balance be right now?

Jesus concludes Matthew 6 by reminding us what to focus our hearts and thoughts on: "So don't worry about having enough food or drink or clothing. Why be like the pagans who are so deeply concerned about these things? Your heavenly Father already knows all your needs, and he will give you all you need from day to day if you live for him and make the Kingdom of God your primary concern" (vv. 31–33).

I realize I must lift my greedy eyes and set them on heaven if I am to move past my strong impulse to take, hold, and hoard for myself. When we're green-eyed greedy guts, failing to view God or money with an eternal focus, we eat the world up rather than bear fruit that blesses others (Matt. 13:22). We shortchange others and ourselves with our stinginess.

Jesus revealed Yahweh's divine savings plan for accumulating treasure in heaven: giving. However, I've found giving is not just a means to raise my future standard of living, but a means to raise my current standard of being. Giving raises my eyes *and* my character at the moment I release the gift. So my tendency to "have eyes bigger than my stomach" becomes a good thing when I'm walking through life with generous eyes.

Yahweh Sisters have eyes bigger than their stomachs and don't bat a lash at sharing their salad with someone in need. Who will you bless today?

BIBLE STUDY

Read chapters 8 and 9 from 2 Corinthians—it'll take only five minutes or so to read all of both. In chapter 8, you'll notice Paul is bragging to the church in Corinth about churches in Macedonia. Then in chapter 9, he tells them that he's also been bragging about them to the Macedonian churches. What's all the bragging about? *Giving*.

Answer the questions below about these chapters.

2 Corinthians 8

1. What kind of situation does Paul say the Macedonians were in when they chose to act generously (v. 2)? What is joyful generosity *not* dependent on?

2. Did they feel pressured into giving this large sum? How do you typically feel when someone's need is made evident to you or you're asked for a financial contribution?

3. What do you see in verse 5 that helped the Macedonian churches respond as they did?

4. German poet Johann Wolfgang von Goethe advised, "Don't

say that you want to give, but go ahead and give! You'll never catch up with a mere hope." The poet sounds like Paul in his advice to Corinth from verse 11. Write it in your own words here as a "memo to self."

5. In the next verse (12) Paul points out that it's not so much the amount we give that is crucial but rather our attitude about giving it. Ever feel like it's not worth bothering if you can't give a sizable sum? What other thoughts stop you?

6. Verses 14–15 describe how money should flow among Yahweh Sisters. How is this different from how we live today? Why do you think that is?

2 Corinthians 9

7. In verses 5–7 Paul—echoing Jesus—talks about the connection between our hearts, thoughts, and giving. He doesn't want us giving from compulsion or resentment. Then, in verse 8 a promise is offered. What happens when we give cheerfully?

8. Look in the remaining few paragraphs of chapter 9 and make a list of at least four things that happen when we give (in addition to the glorious fact that we store up treasure for eternity!).

9. Finally, flip over to Luke 12:13–21 to see what Jesus said about those of us with hoarder disorders. Explain.

6

Don't Be Afraid in the Dark

Revealing the Secret of Growth through Trials

Faint rumblings register in my mind. I wonder if it's the activity of a distant neighbor. More sounds, slightly louder, slightly more jarring. I ask my daughter if it's thunder, as she returns from outdoors. "No," she answers decidedly. "It's not going to rain. Not a cloud in the sky."

One glance through the nearby window confirms her forecast: blue skies. I recall my neighbor theory and return to my work at the computer. But not for long.

Within minutes gray clouds roll in overhead with thunderous claps. Lights flicker inside the house as lightning illuminates the landscape. God's creatures scurry for shelter as sheets of water fall forcefully from above.

This is a brutal rain, the kind that comes out of nowhere, knocking petals from blooms and sending young children to hide

under their beds. Day transforms into night—bright sunlight
melding into wet darkness.

In Scripture, the twelve disciples experienced this kind of force-
ful storm. Twice.

Taking on Water

The first storm descended upon the disciples as they sailed with Jesus
on a lake in a wooden craft. "Suddenly, a terrible storm came up, with
waves breaking into the boat" (Matt. 8:24). I grew up spending my
summers on a lake. Few things terrified me like being in a boat in
the middle of that lake when a lightning storm hit. Water sloshing
into your vessel faster than you can bail it out reliably raises the blood
pressure.

The disciples panicked in this situation, despite the fact that
several of them were experienced boaters, career fishermen. They
woke Jesus shouting, "Save us, we're going to drown!" (v. 25). Picture
something along the lines of Discovery Channel's *Deadliest Catch*—
the waves on this lake, called the Sea of Galilee, could reach twenty
feet high!

With sleep clinging to His eyes, Jesus stood from His resting
place to respond to His followers. After questioning their panic and
reminding them of the power of faith, He commanded the wind and
waves to settle down. The turbulent storm ended as fast as it began.
Twelve soggy disciples sat in the boat, in awe.

Iron Chef

The second meteorological surprise attack also occurred on the Sea
of Galilee. The relatively small body of water measures about thirteen

miles long by seven miles wide, but is one hundred and fifty feet deep. It sits well below sea level with mountains surrounding. Storms can break suddenly and violently over the hills, rolling down onto the sea below.

Jesus climbed into a boat on the sea's edge after hearing of the murder of his cousin John the Baptist. The grieving Savior sought solace alone on the lake. Soon people from surrounding villages learned His whereabouts and gathered on the shore. Jesus noticed and responded to them. He rowed ashore to comfort them and heal their sick. Hours passed as He moved among the crowd.

About dinnertime, the disciples approached Jesus suggesting He dismiss the crowd to eat in the villages. "That isn't necessary— you feed them," Jesus replied (Matt. 14:16). Jesus tasked a former doctor, a tax collector, and some fishermen with feeding a crowd of thousands. They had little time and even fewer ingredients to work with: a mere five loaves of bread and two fish. Sounds like an episode of the Food Network's *Dinner: Impossible!*

They grumbled. The Bread of Life wanted to feed and provide for His people, but His disciples didn't care to deal with them—a scenario that repeats itself throughout the ages. Jesus blessed and multiplied the loaves and fishes, miraculously feeding many thousands with the meager portion.

The Bible reveals:

> Immediately after this, Jesus insisted that his disciples get back into the boat and cross to the other side of the lake, while he sent the people home. After sending them home, he went up into

the hills by himself to pray. Night fell while he was
there alone. (Matt. 14:22–23)

Jesus remains on the mountainside. The Twelve are in the boat,
in the middle of the deep, dark lake. Soon gale-force winds kick up
over the sea, stirring the waves like a KitchenAid mixer.

Where is He? they must've demanded.

Will He save us? they likely questioned.

Are we doomed here without Him? they must have wondered.

Hours passed as they wrestled powerful waves, desperate to keep
the boat right side up and emptied of water. It had been a long day
of ministry and crowd management. Followed by a long night of
fighting for their lives against the wind, they likely wondered, *Where
is Jesus when we need Him? Does He not care?*

Sudden Storms

I'm guessing a few storms have unexpectedly darkened your days
before too. One minute life is humming along. The next thing you
know, the pink slip comes. The other driver fails to yield. The weath-
erman calls it a Category 5. You discover his hidden stash. The test
results come back. The rejection letter arrives. A man in uniform
knocks at your door. You feel a lump. Your husband announces he's
no longer in love.

Just like that, the warm sunlight of life melds into wet, tear-
stained darkness. You can't see the sky for the rain, and it feels as if
God is a sea plus a mountain away.

Let me ask, what do you tend to do when darkness descends and
trouble hits? Run for the phone to call a friend? Run for the freezer to

comfort with food? Run for the bed to yank the covers protectively overhead?

Most of us prefer to run—sprinting until we find another sunny spot to stand in. We don't like being in the dark—even less, suffering in the dark.

In the dark we can't see what lies ahead. We realize we're no longer in control—not that we ever are fully in control. After all, God is sovereign. But, at least in the daylight on smooth waters, we can feel that we are. Not so once storms hit.

I've lived through some storms. My mother's death from cancer, seven years with chronic pain from fibromyalgia, climbing out of debt I created—twice. Those are just a few of the hurricanes I've hunkered through. I know what it's like to lose sleep, to be in too much pain to sleep, and to be afraid to sleep because when I wake someone I love may be gone.

Yep, I've bailed water and battled waves throughout the night, wondering when God will show up to rescue me. I know how it feels to be afraid in the dark, to stress myself to sleep, and to crawl from bed with circles under my eyes as dark as the days ahead.

Beautiful Strength

Our skin cells renew themselves in the dark, at night while we sleep. We look more radiant waking from a good night's rest. That's why it's called "beauty sleep." Godly beauty also results from time spent in the dark of our prayer closet, in the midst of our troubles, when we draw close to and lean on Him.

Yahweh Sisters aren't afraid in the dark, for we know we aren't alone. God promised He'll never leave us or abandon us (Heb. 13:5).

Hold on to that powerful promise in your darkest hours, sweet Yahweh Sisters. He remains close, regardless of whether or not we notice Him. In John 1:5, Jesus said, "The light shines through the darkness, and the darkness can never extinguish it."

Remember that Jesus stands beside you right in the middle of your crisis, in the middle of your darkest day. He also stands in the middle of your tomorrow, fully aware of your future.

When we remember this, we actively seek Him. Our focus shifts, slightly but effectually, from our circumstances to our God. We search Him out, opening our eyes to see spiritually. Walker Percy said, "To become aware of the possibility of the search is to be onto something. Not to be onto something is to be in despair."[1]

One of my favorite verses sits late in the book of Isaiah, offering great hope for anyone who's ever found themselves in the dark. Poetically beautiful, it gives us potent reason for rejoicing amidst our trials. In Isaiah 45:3 Yahweh reveals:

> "And I will give you treasures hidden in the
> darkness—secret riches. I will do this so that you
> may know that I am the LORD, the God of Israel,
> the one who calls you by name."

God knows us intimately and calls us by our first name. Nothing that happens to us escapes His knowledge. He never loses track of us, forgets who we are, or misses what's going on in our lives. We may not be able to view the shore beyond the twenty-foot waves, but God hones in on our precise location on that deep, dark lake. He holds the power to stop the storm, as well as to use the storm to stir up glorious things.

We can mine great things from the dark times in our lives— things that may not be discovered any other way. Things like irrepressible hope, unsurpassable peace, inexplicable joy, unfailing comfort, divine endurance, and amazing grace. In Isaiah, God calls these secret riches. How will we discover these treasures lying hidden in the darkness of our trials if we're always running for the light, trying desperately to avoid any testing, suffering, or pain?

From Dirt to Diamonds

What's the oldest thing you own? (And don't tell me it's your husband!) Is it a Victorian house—rich with history? An antique cabinet? Your grandmother's broach?

If you own a diamond, that is likely the oldest thing you own.

Most geologists maintain that the diamonds we find on the earth's surface or through mining are at least three billion years old. I'm not sure how that figure jibes with what biblical scholars believe the earth's age is, but suffice it to say diamonds are super old.

Diamonds were formed a long time ago under harsh circumstances. That rock on your hand or on your grandmother's broach evolved from a simple piece of carbon—black coal, neither shiny nor attractive. But, after spending a good long time under extreme heat and pressure, deep in the darkness surrounded by dirt, stone, and lava in the earth's core, it changed.

Intense pressure and heat transformed it into one of the hardest, strongest, most sought-after materials on earth—prized today for both its beauty and its strength.

Trials do that to us. They harden us. We can either allow them to harden our heart, making us bitter, or we can allow them to strengthen our faith, making us useful to and prized in the kingdom of God.

A woman who has sought God while bailing water through a storm and lived to tell about it can be quite valuable in the kingdom indeed. Paul explains why in 2 Corinthians 1:4–5:

> [God] comforts us in all our troubles so that we can comfort others. When others are troubled, we will be able to give them the same comfort God has given us. You can be sure that the more we suffer for Christ, the more God will shower us with his comfort through Christ.

God's comfort breaks through our despair when we turn to Him. Then we hold out that same comfort—and its source—as we comfort friends in their dark times.

My most powerful avenues of ministry flow from the dark, desperate points in my past when I allowed God to be my storm shelter. I wonder if we sometimes pray for God to strengthen our troubled friends without hearing Him say, "You feed them for me." As we share our stories of God's faithfulness, we feed them the faith we've gained through our trials. That's multiplying the fish and loaves!

A Yahweh Sister who's emerged from the darkness after finding God's comfort is a valuable woman, wife, mother, or friend indeed. Comfort is one of those hidden treasures we desperately need to learn to find in Yahweh, rather than seek through success, cocktails, shopping, affairs, or the pantry. Think how much devastation is caused by anxious, hurting people looking for comfort outside of God.

In John 14:18 Jesus says, "I will not leave you comfortless: I will come to you" (KJV). That's a strong, assertive statement spoken with the authority of God. Believe it, my stressed-out Sisters, and ask for it each time gray clouds start rolling in over your lake.

Peace like a River

Though decades have passed since my mother's death, I still find myself grieving occasionally. No longer at predictable times like Christmas or Mother's Day, but at unexpected times. Like when I reach for a mug and see my mother's hand extended before me. Or I come across something with her handwriting on it. Or my attempts to make her signature recipes fail. These moments send me reeling, once again feeling my loss.

I recall just such a time when I sank to my kitchen floor sobbing over a flopped cake. I felt certain this wouldn't have happened if I'd had a mom around to teach me to bake. I remember this day in great detail because it was the day I discovered that if I call on Jesus in between tearful heaves and ask Him for peace in His name, I can go from crying to calm in a single breath.

After eking out, "Jesus …. Help … I need … Your peace," I experienced the secret riches of divine peace. The rush of peace didn't make me a better cook, but it kept me from crying any longer on the floor. I sat there tear-soggy and awed, just like the disciples in the boat. With my newfound calm, I got up, dumped the flopped cake in a pretty glass bowl, and covered it with Cool Whip. It was delish. (Cool Whip covers a multitude of dessert sins.)

His peace flooded in like a river cresting its banks. That's the power of the God of all comfort. That's the kindness of the Father of compassion. That's the gift from the One who commands the wind—the same One who in His own time of grief got out of the boat to help those aching on the shore. Are you aching today? He will climb out of the boat to rescue you. Call on His name.

In each of my dark times I've met a different aspect of this God: Comforter, Healer, Protector, Provider. Without those trials, I wouldn't have the strength of character and faith I have today. My vault would be devoid of secret riches.

I used to think James surely wrote his epistle before his morning cup of java. Some of his statements seemed foggy-headed notions to me. Now I understand his perplexing urge: "Consider it a sheer gift, friends, when tests and challenges come at you from all sides. You know that under pressure, your faith-life is forced into the open and shows its true colors. So don't try to get out of anything prematurely. Let it do its work so you become mature and well-developed, not deficient in any way" (James 1:2–4 MSG).

Irrepressible hope, unsurpassable peace, inexplicable joy, unfailing comfort, patient endurance, and amazing grace await us in the dark times if we'll seek Him in them. Finding these treasures, we experience calm despite the storm. We develop spiritual beauty and spiritual strength—and others are drawn to us in their own times of need.

That piece of coal-turned-diamond drawing stares in the jewelry store window is so brilliant that it's hard to imagine its dark, dingy origin. It'd still be dirty and rough if a master gemologist hadn't put his hand to it—cutting it, shaping it, and polishing it to become the valuable, light-reflecting stone we see today.

So it is with our trials. They're intense, and often last longer than we think we can endure. It hurts when God uses His shaping and buffing tools on our lives via our trials. Yet we can emerge stronger, more beautiful, more Christ-reflecting, and more valuable to God and the Sisterhood as a result.

That makes Yahweh Sisters some seriously wealthy women.

Walking on Faith

The disciples were in the throes of their second big storm—wet, weary, and barely thinking straight. The time? About 3:00 a.m.

Already unnerved, they grew frightened when past the boat's edge they saw a figure moving toward them on the water. They feared it was a ghost until he spoke with the familiar voice of their Rabbi. Jesus assured, "It's all right…. I am here! Don't be afraid" (Matt. 14:27).

Peter replied, "Lord, if it's really you, tell me to come to you by walking on the water" (v. 28). Interestingly, walking on the water was Peter's idea. Peter displayed logic-bending faith as he tells Jesus to speak forth his ability to do so. "All right, come," Jesus responded (v. 29). Adding action to his faith, Peter climbed out of the vessel. In the margin of my Bible I wrote beside Peter's statement, "Anything Jesus says is possible!"

Peter was the only one in the boat with enough faith to relax in the middle of the stormy night and trust Christ with the outcome. Throwing one leg over the side, he shifted his body weight onto murky moving liquid. As he did, he found a hidden treasure in that troubled night. He discovered he could do all things—amazing

things, impossible things—through Christ who strengthened him
(see Phil. 4:13).

Out on the shifting waves, Peter kept his eyes on Jesus. As long
as he focused on the Lord, Peter's faith remained strong and his body
suspended over the depths. He placed one human foot after the
other on top of common seawater—and walked nearer to the heart
of God. When Peter looked away from Jesus to the winds whipping
all around, his faith faltered. He started going under.

The story continues:

> Instantly Jesus reached out his hand and grabbed
> him. "You don't have much faith," Jesus said. "Why
> did you doubt me?" And when they climbed back
> into the boat, the wind stopped. Then the disciples
> worshiped him. "You really are the Son of God!"
> they exclaimed. (Matt. 14:31–33)

Notice the wind stopped right after they climbed back in the boat.
Park your mind on that fact a moment. What does it tell you?

Jesus knew His crew feared the storm. He could've calmed the
wind from the mountainside where He was praying. He could've
stopped the squall from the shore before He set foot on the waves.
But He had something amazing to show them.

Jesus can calm the storms in our lives with a simple command.
Sometimes He does; other times He has something He wants
us to see first. There is something He hopes we'll experience first.
Something He hopes we'll find—something that will strengthen our
faith and others'.

The tempest didn't cease until after Peter experienced the miracle of walking on wind-whipped water—an incident he'd remember and teach about for the rest of his life. Indeed, an occurrence that convinced everyone in the boat that Jesus *is* the Son of God. We still marvel at this miracle today.

John Ortberg writes, "Getting out of the boat was Peter's great gift to Jesus; the experience of walking on water was Jesus' great gift to Peter."[2] In that damp darkness, Peter learned things about his God, his faith, and himself that he wouldn't have discovered under sunny skies on terra firma.

Yahweh Sisters, next time we hear the rumbling of thunder clouds rolling in, or feel the pelt of rain on our shoulders, let's not panic or run frantically. Rather, let's trust God will see us through the storm, and ask Him to show us the secret riches He has waiting in the darkness.

What gift might be wrapped and waiting there with your name on it?

BIBLE STUDY

1. Eugene Peterson renders 2 Corinthians 1:3–5 (MSG) like this:

> All praise to the God and Father of our Master, Jesus the Messiah! Father of all mercy! God of all healing counsel! He comes alongside us when we go through hard times, and before you know it, he

brings us alongside someone else who is
going through hard times so that we can
be there for that person just as God was
there for us. We have plenty of hard times
that come from following the Messiah,
but no more so than the good times of his
healing comfort—we get a full measure of
that, too.

Recall and write down a time when God helped you through
a trial.

Pray for opportunities to come alongside someone else and
share this story.

2. God loves to bring light out of the darkness! Read three
   instances of that and make notes.
   Genesis 1:1–5

   Matthew 4:12–17

   Mark 15:33–37

3. Read Proverbs 29:25, Proverbs 30:5, and Matthew 10:28–31. What reasons do you glean from these passages for fearing nothing but the power of God?

4. The Proverbs 31 woman is described in verse 25: "She is clothed with strength and dignity; and she laughs with no fear of the future." What do you imagine allows her to have such little fear that she can laugh when trials come her way?

Paul gives us insight into that ability in James 1:2–4 and 1 Peter 4:12–13. Read these and explain below why you can choose to rejoice rather than panic when troubles hit.

7

Adjust your Scale

Revealing the Secret of Perfection in God's Eyes

I see the annoying thing hanging in the doctor's office. Other times I spot it while flipping through a magazine in the checkout aisle. I already know what it's going to say about me, but I still read it. Sadly, the height-weight chart tells me I don't measure up to my ideal.

My own bathroom scale conspires with the chart, regularly confirming what I already know. Even when I shed every stitch of clothing first. Even first thing in the morning when I haven't eaten anything yet. Note that these are the only conditions under which I willingly weigh myself. Sometimes I exhale fully before quickly stepping on the platform. No matter my tricks, the scale has told me for years that I'm nowhere near perfect.

A bit of an optimist, I never give up hope that one day I'll reach the published ideal, or at least come really close. (What's five or seven pounds among friends?) I head for the treadmill, mindful of a few pieces of clothing saved at the back of my closet with the target number on their labels. I can't be the only gal whose hope of perfection remains woven into the fabric of some article of clothing.

My quest for perfection doesn't stop in my closet, or my bathroom mirror. It extends beyond my physical appearance to encompass every role in life—cooking, cleaning, parenting, writing, teaching, marriage, ministry, etc. My thought process has long been *why settle for average when you can shoot for perfection?*

Don't let me mislead you into thinking that I work super hard at being perfect in every area of my life. I don't, and my life attests to that fact. I often slack off or procrastinate. I grow distracted, exhausted, or overwhelmed and don't do my best. Then I beat myself up with regret because my actions, efforts, or outcomes don't match the idealized image in my head.

Oftentimes I do work hard, giving it my all, and yet I still don't measure up to my mental ideal. Then I grow self-critical, frustrated, or insecure. Case in point: As I complete most chapters of this book, the notion that I could've done better overshadows my feelings of accomplishment.

I reckon I frustrate others with my lack of perfection. I imagine Rick wants a perfect wife. Surely, my kids would prefer a perfect mom. No doubt my students would benefit from a perfect teacher. Don't my readers deserve a perfect example? Because I want to be perfect, I imagine those around me wish I were perfect. I reason surely God wants me to be perfect too.

I thought I'd found proof of that when I read the verse where Jesus said, "But you are to be perfect, even as your Father in heaven is perfect" (Matt. 5:48). I had two reactions to this verse: First, I wanted to know how to accomplish this perfection He spoke of; and second, I felt guilty for not measuring up to it before now!

The Merriam-Webster online dictionary defines perfect as "being entirely without fault or defect, satisfying all requirements, or corresponding to an ideal standard."[1] I know I'm not the only Yahweh Sister who wants to reach this status. Am I, girls?

Role Models

The problem is this definition cannot describe me, you, or any other woman. It describes God alone. Even the biblical characters we hold in high regard or heroes of the faith—like missionaries and martyrs—cannot be described as "entirely without fault or defect." Read a few history books, and you'll realize this. Open the pages of the Bible, and you'll see evidence of imperfection.

Disobedient Adam and Eve ate the apple. Cain killed Abel. Noah got drunk and passed out, naked no less. Abraham lied about his wife, twice—didn't he learn his lesson? Sarah mistreated Hagar. Lot's wife looked back, leaving her daughters motherless. Rebekah deceived her husband and favored one son over the other. Jacob stole his brother's birthright. Rachel stole her father's idols. Leah and Rachel fought like cats. Joseph's jealous brothers sold him into slavery. And that's just the beginning—all are examples from the book of Genesis. The Bible continues like this all the way to Revelation. No person in between the sacred pages—saint or sinner—was perfect, except for Jesus.

That's why Christ should be our primary role model. However, if you're like me, you have a tendency to try to conform to any number of additional role models. Fitness experts. Financial gurus. Best-selling diet doctors. Creative mavens. Fashionistas. Successful entrepreneurs. Celebrity chefs. Actresses. Productivity specialists. These people may have something helpful to teach us, or something inspiring to glean, but they are not perfect.

Martha Stewart's name has long been associated with perfection. She cooks, cleans, organizes, decorates, entertains, and crafts with seeming superhero power. She also sells goods and runs a multifaceted, multibillion dollar corporation. Through her books, magazines, and television shows, she sets the standard for domestic flawlessness.

However, even the great Martha Stewart is not perfect. She's had trouble maintaining quality relationships within her home and business. She's divorced. Oh, and there's also that matter of her going to jail for obstruction of justice over some financial dealings. Beyond the beautifully crafted Cape Cod facade lays imperfection.

That's OK, we reason, because we'll just follow her advice about homemaking, Dr. Phil's advice regarding relationships, and Suze Orman's advice on finances. Oh sure, conforming to the advice of multiple experts can be a lot to manage, but doing so will lead us to a better life, right? Combining these role models' various strengths will make us ideal women.

Better Living

I recently stumbled upon a curious blog by Robyn Okrant. At the age of thirty-five, Okrant set out to follow *all* the advice given on the *Oprah Show* for an entire year and blog about her experiences during the challenge. In 2008 she kept a running list from each episode of all the things Oprah and her guests said people must do or have. She tackled that to-do list like a charter member of Perfectionists-R-Us.

This woman was committed! If Oprah's show said every room should have a funky, cool chair, she bought a funky, cool chair. If the show told her she should have her doctor run a certain test to check for a certain ailment, she made the appointment. When the show told her to rescue a pet from a shelter, she adopted a cat and named it Oprah. If the show introduced a new recipe, Okrant cooked it. Any books Oprah endorsed, Okrant read. She spent thousands of dollars purchasing "the good life according to Oprah." She even bought a recommended backyard fire pit and ergonomic garden tools—even though she has no yard.

I thought her a bit crazy, but still I was intrigued by her project. I spot-read through some of the year's posts, and then headed for her December entries, to see her conclusions.

Had doing this improved her life? Would she keep it up? Was she a better woman for it? For a brief moment somewhere in a recessed corner of my mind, I actually wondered if I, too, should try this. And I don't even watch *Oprah*.

Her December posts revealed a woman too burnt-out to accurately or objectively assess her year just yet. She blearily stumbled across her December 31 finish line. On January 1, 2009, she wrote: "I did cross everything off my Oprah to-do list. I cannot believe it. That makes me misty thinking about it. And then I start to think I'm a jerk for feeling so emotional about a self-imposed project such as this. I keep wavering back and forth between feeling AWESOME and FOOLISH. Clearly, I need a full night's sleep and some soul-searching."

Okrant told *Today Show* host Matt Lauer, "I think I'm an example of how ridiculous it gets when women follow icons or follow celebrities completely, so I know there's a shade of the absurd in here. I am not an Oprah fanatic. Oprah's like the popular girl in high school, and she tells us what to do and how to dress and we do it, and we're happy because of it."

However, happiness eluded Okrant come December. Instead of feeling blissful, she felt exhausted. Why are we so easily trapped by the idea that following all the right advice will bring perfection and therefore happiness? When asked if she'd recommend other people try her better-living-through-Oprah project, Okrant replied, "No, no, no—run the opposite way!"

Yahweh Sisters, why do we even hesitate to run the opposite way? Why do we stray from the divine plan of better living through God's grace? There are no required products to buy, and there's only one book to read.

We've been conditioned to earn our way, to perform correctly, to not make mistakes. We seek love and respect from God and others through what we do and how well we do it. In turn, we expect others to earn our love and respect. To a degree, we even expect God to earn it by blessing us with "the good life" so long as we behave well.

If we live this way, we operate from a performance-based perspective. Performance-based love holds up many high standards, granting love only when all conditions are met. In other words, love must be earned. The source of love becomes our ability to impress.

Jesus shows us a new perspective: grace-based love. Grace-based love rejects the earning paradigm—that was the old system, the Old Testament, the old covenant. Grace-based love finds its source in

God. It holds up the cross and grants love before anyone returns the affection. We don't earn it; we receive it. First-century Christians in Galatia learned a thing or two about this.

Some Kind of Crazy

In ancient Galatia, radically conservative Jewish leaders insisted that new Christians, including the Gentile converts, follow *all* the Jewish laws. Jewish law was made up of three parts: civil, ceremonial, and moral. We're talking more than six hundred laws!

God gave the moral laws to Moses and the prophets. The moral law was God's bottom line—think the Ten Commandments. The many Jewish civil and ceremonial laws encompassed regulations about how Jews should conduct themselves daily. Like rules for how worship services should go.… (Hmmm, come to think of it, the hoopla over that issue continues in the church today.) Or what, where, when, and with whom to eat—nonessentials in light of the new covenant Christ ushered in. Think funky-chair, no-white-shoes-after-Labor-Day, or buy-only-ergonomic-garden-tools advice. While these may have some merit, they're not what ultimately concern God's heart.

Jesus calls for continued obedience to the moral laws. He clarifies, "Don't misunderstand why I have come. I did not come to abolish the law of Moses or the writings of the prophets. No, I came to fulfill them" (Matt. 5:17). While fulfilling all of the laws, which ultimately led to His becoming the sacrifice on our behalf, Jesus ushered in a new order, a higher order. An order of grace and love.

Salvation doesn't flow from our good deeds. It cannot be earned. I think we mostly get that. But we tend to think our good deeds cause God to love us more.

They don't.

Surprised?

God is love. It is His very essence. We must keep this in the forefront of our performance-based minds. God's love for us doesn't evolve from any particular thing about who we are—how we look, what grades we earn, how many committees we're on, or if we pass the bell-ringer outside Walmart at Christmas without dropping in change. Rather, God's love finds its source in Him and who He is. It's directed at us.

Yahweh loves us because love is what He is and what He does. We are His creation. We belong to Him. He loved us long before we ever returned that love or offered Him an ounce of worship (1 John 4:19). And He will love us should we neglect offering any thanks or praise to Him today. Does that bother you at all? I'll admit that truth sometimes gets under my performance-based skin!

Trying to keep all the nonessential laws and earn God's love through good works had long been a heavy yoke around Israel's neck. And suddenly the Jewish leaders insisted the Gentile Christians wear it as well. (Isn't that always the case? We want others to jump through the same hoops we do, to care about the same things we care about, to conform to our definition of perfect.)

How did the new Christians in Galatia respond? Like they'd been following self-help programs and writing to-do lists all their lives. They set out to earn God's favor and perfect themselves by keeping the regulations to a T. They switched the scale from God's grace-based love, offered in Christ, to their own human performance. Paul corrects them in Galatians 3:1–5 (MSG):

You crazy Galatians! Did someone put a hex on you? Have you taken leave of your senses? Something crazy has happened, for it's obvious that you no longer have the crucified Jesus in clear focus in your lives. His sacrifice on the cross was certainly set before you clearly enough.

Let me put this question to you: How did your new life begin? Was it by working your heads off to please God? Or was it by responding to God's Message to you? *Are you going to continue this craziness? For only crazy people would think they could complete by their own efforts what was begun by God. If you weren't smart enough or strong enough to begin it, how do you suppose you could perfect it?* Did you go through this whole painful learning process for nothing? It is not yet a total loss, but it certainly will be if you keep this up!

Answer this question: Does the God who lavishly provides you with his own presence, his Holy Spirit, working things in your lives you could never do for yourselves, does he do these things because of your strenuous moral striving or because you trust him to do them in you?

Paul's words hit a perfectionistic gal right in the gut, don't they? This passage makes me ask, *Do I allow God to perfect me and others, or do I insist on doing it myself?* Yahweh Sisters, it's time to check our scales:

- Do we love and judge ourselves or others based solely on performance?
- Do we believe in our heart, or with our actions, that God loves us more when we don't mess up?
- Do we expect others to conform to our particular notion of ideal?
- Do we withhold our love until people conform or measure up in our eyes?

Switching Scales

But what about that Matthew 5:48 verse where Jesus told us to be perfect like God? Is that not a mandate from Christ for total perfection? Before you go on a cleaning, organizing, strict diet, exercise, Bible study binge, let's look at the definition and context of this verse. That's where I discovered the secret to perfection in God's eyes.

The word *perfect* used in this verse means "complete, full grown, developing" in the ancient Greek language. The first two pieces of that definition are different from the third. The first two indicate something already accomplished, while the third indicates an ongoing process. Somehow this perfection is both already complete and yet still developing.

All parts of the definition, however, refer to maturity of character rather than flawless execution of all behaviors. Jesus wants us to excel at doing good—excel at keeping God's moral law just as He did. But let's be honest, that's often not what we're trying to excel at. We're busy trying to keep our appearance, performance, surroundings, and circumstances up to the level we imagine they should be. We're trying to make everything appear perfect to please ourselves, our friends, or society. Too often, God's priorities and ours differ.

Was Jesus a perfectionist? Depends on your definition of the term. Jesus was not a nitpicky dude.

Think about it—when Jesus told His disciples to drop their nets in the sea, and they caught so many fish their nets nearly burst, did He critique the way they'd knotted their ropes? When asked to turn water into wine for a wedding celebration run dry, did Jesus criticize the host for poor event planning? When He told Zaccheus to climb down from the tree and take Him home for dinner, did Jesus gasp at Zaccheus' short stature or care if his house was company-ready? No, Jesus stayed focused on the big picture of maturing people's faith and character. He didn't major in the minor aspects of appearance, possessions, or performance.

Jesus told busy-in-the-kitchen Martha that only one thing was required. It wasn't floors so spotless you could eat off them. It wasn't a tuna-noodle casserole with the cheese baked evenly on top and no crunchy, burnt noodles on the sides. It wasn't Christmas cards featuring a family photo with everyone matching and smiling, mailed out the first day of December. It wasn't to sell more real estate than any other Realtor in town. It wasn't to be so organized you can put your french-manicured hands on your birth certificate in a moment's notice. It wasn't to air out your down comforter twice a year, or make your bed each morning with "hospital corners." It wasn't to always fit into your wedding dress, or even to get married. The one thing required was to allow God's grace and truth into your heart to shape your character.

When we look at the context of this verse, we learn another key to perfection in God's eyes. Jesus spoke this verse during His Sermon on the Mount. It comes within His teaching on Jewish law, sandwiched between the Beatitudes and the Lord's Prayer. Read it in context:

> "You have heard the law that says, 'Love your neighbor' and hate your enemy. But I say, love your enemies! Pray for those who persecute you! In that way, you will be acting as true children of your Father in heaven. For he gives his sunlight to both the evil and the good, and he sends rain on the just and the unjust alike. If you love only those who love you, what good is that? Even corrupt tax collectors do that much. If you are kind only to your friends, how are you different from anyone else? Even pagans do that. But you are to be perfect, even as your Father in heaven is perfect." (Matt. 5:43–48)

Matthew Henry, in his *Concise Commentary on the Whole Bible*, wrote this about this passage:

> The Jewish teachers by "neighbour" understood only those who were of their own country, nation, and religion, whom they were pleased to look upon as their friends. The Lord Jesus teaches that we must do all the real kindness we can to all, especially

to their souls. We must pray for them.... Others salute their brethren, and embrace those of their own party, and way, and opinion, but we must not so confine our respect. It is the duty of Christians to desire, and aim at, and press toward *perfection in grace and holiness*. And therein we must study to conform ourselves to the example of our heavenly Father.[2]

So Jesus' statement to be perfect like God comes in the context of loving others who are not like us: foreigners, strangers, even enemies. We are called to love those who don't love us. Love those who don't live up to our expectations or meet our standards. Those who look differently. Those who do things totally differently than we do. Those who don't value the same things we value. Those who don't appear to measure up socially, economically, or on the height-weight charts of life.

Quite often, I actually find it easier to offer love and grace to those radically different from me. Where I struggle most is granting grace and love to those closest to me: friends, family, and Yahweh Sisters who are similar to me but don't behave exactly how I think they should. Perfectionistic gals like me apply their notion of ideal (their particular brand of crazy) to everyone around them, growing angry when others fail to live up.

Do you live with some of these similar-but-not-measuring-up people too? You know, those who don't have the good sense to wipe or remove their muddy shoes before walking on your carpet. Those who don't bother to sort darks from lights when doing laundry.

Those who leave the cap off the soda pop so it goes flat. And those who habitually run late. We assume these people should know better—*we've taught them how to do things right!* Being perfect as God is perfect has nothing to do with maintaining a flawless home, wardrobe, figure, or track record. It's about giving and receiving love ... giving and receiving grace ... just as God does.

By the way, this also means granting yourself grace, just like God does.

Step Off the Treadmill

How do we muster the power to love when staring at muddy footprints in the carpet or the white socks now pink? How do we grant grace when someone drops the ball or opposes us at work? We can't, at least not consistently. Not with willpower alone.

Grace and love flow from God to us, and then it's available to flow through us to others. Paul told the Galatians the same thing. Maturing isn't something you manage to do for God; it's what you allow God to do through you. It's the difference between having a heart for God, and having God's own heart.

Allowing God to do the work of grace in and through us gets us off that stressful treadmill of performance. Stepping down from the spinning deck, we experience freedom, relief, and gratefulness. We receive rest and grace. This experience enables us to let others step down from the performance deck as well.

What a tremendous secret grace-based love is! What an absolute gift to be free from the relentless standards of performance-based love. What a relief that perfection is about maturing in character, and that we're not solely responsible for accomplishing it. Rather, Christ and the Holy Spirit working in us "perfected forever all those whom he is making holy" (Heb. 10:14).

What a relief, and yet what a discipline it is to grant grace to ourselves and others—including, if not especially, in the nonessential, burnt-tuna-casserole, running-late, laundry-washing-debacle things of daily life.

Sweet Sisters, we must understand the part of us that strives for relentless perfection and bring it under the influence of truth and grace. Let's temper it, and direct it. Focus it on motives and character more so than performance and image. Let's let Jesus' definition of *perfect* shape and channel our own.

Living in God's Reality

I'll still look to the height-weight chart for a healthy ideal, but I hereby resign from the Perfectionists-R-Us Club. I'm handing in my membership card and my performance-based scale. I refuse to continue conforming to the world's many fickle standards when only one thing is required.

Jesus teaches I will not find my worth in my ability to accomplish my to-do list flawlessly, but in the fact that I am a child of God learning to give and receive grace, give and receive love. Yahweh Sisters, let's stop basing our worth on the distance between our actions and our imagined ideals—no matter how large or small that distance is. Instead, we will weigh our worth on scales of grace.

As John writes in 1 John 3:18–19 (MSG): "My dear children, let's not just talk about love; let's practice real love. This is the only way we'll know we're living truly, living in God's reality. It's also the way to shut down debilitating self-criticism, even when there is something to it."

BIBLE STUDY

1. Read Romans 8:1–8. Focus on verse 1 for a minute. What do you condemn about yourself or your performance in life?

   What do you condemn about your loved ones and their performance in life?

   Are these things sin issues or nonessentials in the eyes of God? Explain.

   Regardless, what do verses 1–4 say about them?

   Now focus on verses 4–8. Look these up in *The Message* translation—you can find it online at BibleGateway.com. Part of it says: "Obsession with self in these matters is a dead end; attention to God leads us out into the open, into a spacious, free life. Focusing on the self is the opposite of focusing on God. Anyone completely absorbed in self ignores God, ends up thinking more about self than God. That person ignores who God is and what he is doing. And God isn't pleased at being ignored."

Does your quest for perfection generally lead you toward God or away from Him? What about your loved ones—has your desire for perfection led them any closer to you or to God? Explain.

2. Read 1 John 3:2–3, 1 Corinthians 13:12, and Philippians 3:20-21. What is the prerequisite for being perfected? When will the maturing process God began in you be completed?

3. Colossians 4:5–6 (MSG) says: "Use your heads as you live and work among outsiders. Don't miss a trick. Make the most of every opportunity. Be gracious in your speech. The goal is to bring out the best in others in a conversation, not put them down, not cut them out." Write down what this says to you about how you should treat unbelievers and outsiders—really, anyone that's not measuring up to your standards.

4. Read the book of Jonah—it is short and will take only a few minutes. While most people recall this as a story of a prophet disobeying God and winding up in the belly of a fish, it's also a story about learning to love and extend grace to those different from us: foreigners, sinners, enemies. This book of the Bible ends with a question—record your answer to that question here.

8

Get By with a Little Help from your Friends

Revealing the Secret of Interdependence

I peered across the room to read the alarm clock—2:00 a.m. After stretching and fluffing my pillow, I couldn't get back to sleep.

Deciding drastic measures were needed, I shuffled to the kitchen to fix a cup of Sleepytime tea. Then I broke out the big guns: cinnamon graham crackers. *Surely I can induce sleep with a sugar-chamomile fog.*

Nope.

As I lay awake, an idea struck me. Maybe God wanted my attention, to tell me something. It isn't often that God wakes me in the middle of the night with something to say, but it has happened. Lest you think me super-spiritual, Rick says it's because during the day God has trouble getting a word in edgewise.

I got out my Bible, excited for whatever God wanted to show me. I went to Him in prayer. Then I read. I concentrated. I prayed again. I tried to stay open to His nudge. Looking for something to stand out on the page, I tried to sense some impression in my heart.

Nothing. *Nada*. Zilch. All I sensed was the need for warm milk.

Over an hour passed, and I grew frustrated. Feeling the urge to eat every sweet, salty, or mayonnaise-laden thing in the fridge, I headed for the couch instead.

I scanned the TV channels. Not a lot on in the middle of the night unless you're obsessed with buying kitchen gadgets off infomercials. Then I caught a glimpse of Sandra Bullock. The movie in progress was *28 Days*. I realized Sandra wasn't playing her usual comedic character but a woman with a drinking problem, in denial about it, and sentenced to twenty-eight days in a rehab center.

It wasn't what I'd call a feel-good movie. Nor would it win any awards for Christian programming. Nonetheless, I watched.

What's Your Sign?

When Sandra's character, Gwen, enters the rehab center, she's introduced to various people. Each of the characters at the rehab center—like each of us—has their own addictions, issues, quirks, and charms.

One woman in particular, a minor character, stood out to me. When Gwen meets her, she's sitting with the group, wearing a sign around her neck. Just a handmade sign. It read:

Confront me if I don't ask for help.

I wondered about that sign until Sandra's character later struggled with an issue and a counselor wrote it on poster board, making
her wear it around her neck until she dealt with it. Evidently the
woman I noticed had trouble asking others for help when she needed
it, leading her to feel overwhelmed and retreat into substance abuse.

When the movie drew to a close, I asked myself why I watched
it. Then I asked God the same question, and He nudged me about
the woman with the sign. *Can you imagine wearing that sign, Rachel?*

As I crawled back in bed, I imagined it, all right—I think I had a
nightmare! That week I talked to my friends about it and discovered
we all dislike asking for help. We hate asking for it almost as much as
we hate needing it. And, mercy, do we dislike needing it!

Sign, Sign, Everywhere a Sign

Why are we all so afraid to share our troubles with one another and
ask for aid? Do we imagine we're the only ones with problems? Or
that ours are so much worse than theirs? Are we comparing our *I'm-
stuck* insides with everyone else's *I'm-fine* outsides?

The temptation is to quickly read those questions I just asked,
feel a shred of identification, and move on. We're just not certain
the benefits of asking for help are worth the risk. So pause and truly
consider this issue. Do a little self-examination. What is holding you
back when you find yourself in need of help yet refusing to ask for it?

Here is a list of reasons why I hesitate to ask for help. See if you
can relate to any.

- Pride—It's too humbling or humiliating to admit I
  need help.
- Fear—What if they ignore me, laugh, or reject my request?

- Insecurity—Everyone is too busy to help someone like me.
- Self-Reliance—I think I'm perfectly capable to go at this alone.
- Perfectionism—It will turn out better if I do it myself.
- Busyness—It will take more time to involve others, and I'm already short on time.
- Selfishness—If I ask for help now, I'll be compelled to return the favor someday, and I don't want to owe anyone anything.

Which excuses plague you? Are there other reasons you avoid seeking support?

Not only do we each have problems and excuses for why we keep them to ourselves, but we all have some form of help to offer the Sisterhood. Paul explains, "A spiritual gift is given to each of us as a means of helping the entire church" (1 Cor. 12:7).

That's the purpose of the gifts and talents God has given you—to help others. Ditto for them—their gifts are there to help you. God created the members of the body of Christ, the church, to need and to help one another.

One friend recently confessed to me, "I think my biggest struggle in this area is that I never want to be an obligation to anyone … ever. I will think 'now does she feel obligated to help me, or does she really want to?' Useless, pitiful thinking, I know. But it's my main struggle!" I can relate to my friend's "pitiful" thinking because I often feel that way too.

I want everyone to like me; therefore, I never want to impose on them with my problems. My *aha!* moment came when I realized God hardwired us to need one another and gifted us to help one another.

God may want that person to help me today, whether they feel like it or not. Refusing to ask them deprives them of their opportunity to serve, of an opportunity to fulfill *their* purpose.

Yahweh Sisters, if we're not offering and receiving help from one another, we're not fulfilling our purpose. We're missing out on an important part of Christian community and robbing others of their chance to use their gifts to God's glory.

We Are Family

God is a community of Father, Son, and Holy Spirit. As Yahweh Sisters, we're folded into that community. Look at the pronouns used in Genesis when God says, "Let *us* make people in *our* image, to be like *ourselves*" (1:26). Amazingly, the three-part God made us to be in community together with Him. At no point is isolation or self-sufficiency God's plan—we need others!

You're probably thinking, *But Rachel, being in community can be such a hassle—people drive me nuts!* You're right, it can, and they do. The trick is to realize that and be OK with it anyway. Expect it. That's what community is about: Knowing people and loving them anyway. Being fully known, and yet fully loved.

What we have to keep in mind whenever we are dealing with people is we're all a little bit crazy! This is true of the people you live with, work with, socialize with, serve with, and go to church with. I ike to say we all have a little Lucille Ball in us. So let's stop wasting precious energy pretending otherwise.

We've all got our issues, our baggage experiences, our pet peeves, our weaknesses, our harebrained ideas, our nutty hang-ups and quirks, and areas of our character that God is still working on. That's just the way it is on this side of eternity. So we have to be willing to freely give and receive grace and to give and receive help. Because when we don't, people wind up isolated, hurting, and wondering if it's worth the risk to connect with others.

Friends Don't Let Friends Fall

Last autumn I spent a weekend among the redwoods in the mountains of Santa Cruz with some terrific Sisters in Christ. On Saturday, the retreat center ropes course opened during the afternoon. I couldn't wait to sign up.

Hiking up the steep hillside in the late-day sun, I craned my neck, squinting to spot the cable I'd just paid twenty dollars for the opportunity to walk upon. It was high up, punctuated with obstacles, and much narrower than I expected.

Butterflies hatched in my mind and took flight in my stomach. As I looked around the giant trees, I suddenly questioned my safety, my ability to be successful, and my sanity. After all, the only other people taking this challenge were a few able-bodied teens and a former Hollywood stuntwoman!

I listened intently as the course instructor taught us how to put on and use our safety equipment. I rested easier after she double-checked my harness. Then I began my ascent.

Climbing the rope ladder wasn't hard, given the adrenaline surging through my veins. Nor was my initial short trek across the wire from the first tree to the second. I placed one foot in front of the other, with extreme concentration and caution. I felt every muscle in my body tense. *Surely I'll relax into this as the course progresses.*

Nope.

I and my muscles remained tense and grew weary. And the course didn't get easier, but more challenging. By the time I reached the last half of the most difficult leg at the end, I wondered if I would make it without falling.

If I fell, I would not hit the ground. At some point soon the harness would stop my descent. I knew that full well. Still, every instinctive fiber in my being shouted, "DO. NOT. FALL!"

At one point I suspected I wasn't going to make it and thought of that sign from *28 Days*. I didn't want to ask for help. Nor did I want to be the one who fell. Others had successfully finished the course ahead of me. Still others were watching from the ground and taking pictures. *Do I play it cool, or do I admit I'm in trouble?* I wondered as sweat drenched my forehead.

I called to my course instructor, waiting a few yards away on a tree-mounted platform and confessed I was growing tired and unsure. She stepped out on the wire and headed toward me. I expected her to take my hand or throw me a rope. Instead, she moved in close, smiled, and told me to take a step toward her.

Once I did, she took a step away from me. Cruel, right? She continued this until I reached the platform. Though she never touched me, she did help me across that wire. Her nearness, her confidence in me, and her words of encouragement did more to soothe my psyche than knowing I wore a harness that would break my fall if I slipped.

The reward for all this self-inflicted stress? Jumping off that platform and flying fifty feet down the zip line between the majestic redwoods to the ground below. *Whoo hoo,* that part was worth it. So was learning that I could handle more than I realized with encouragement from a sister who had walked this path before me.

Lend Me Your Hand

The surprising thing about redwoods is, though they tower as high as the Statue of Liberty and often grow as big around as a Greyhound bus, their roots are shallow. Many trees put down roots ten to fifteen feet deep. Redwoods, however, go down maybe six feet.

How do the red giants remain standing with such shallow roots? They grow together in clumps, intertwining their roots with others as far away as two hundred feet. Each one is an individual beauty, yet connected with the others for survival. Even the tallest trees are held up by the smallest ones. By holding hands underground, they hold each other up in the storms of life.

I think that's an apt picture of the body of Christ. We have to lend each other a hand, or an eye, or a foot …

> The human body has many parts, but the many parts make up one body. So it is with the body of Christ…. and [God] has put each part just where he wants it. What a strange thing a body would be if it had only one part! Yes, there are many parts, but only one body. The eye can never say to the hand, "I don't need you." The head can't say to the feet, "I don't need you." (1 Cor. 12:12, 18–21)

We're each a part of the body of Christ—some of us are eyes with the gift of vision, others are feet with the ability to mobilize into action. The eyes can't move without the feet. The feet don't know where to head without the eyes. We're each gifted to meet the others' needs.

Since watching the movie *28 Days*, I frequently think about the woman with the "ask for help" sign. Her sign now hangs in my mind, reminding me to lay aside my pride and seek help when I'm stuck.

Here's Your Sign

My husband, Rick, has a different "ask for help" sign. He carries it with him daily in his left hand. Let me explain.

A crape myrtle tree grows next to our house, shading our driveway. It blooms gloriously all summer. However, wet limbs laden with flowers scrape our car tops, forcing Rick to trim the branches periodically.

One sticky hot summer day Rick used a stepladder to cut back the branches over the driveway. Then he decided to do more trimming above. He hoisted himself from the ladder top onto the lower portion of our roof over the porch. Normally Rick uses a second-floor window to step out onto the porch roof, but that day he climbed to the roof from the ladder on a whim.

Once done pruning, Rick realized he couldn't see the ladder below to get down. He considered knocking on the bedroom window for me to come open it for him, but he didn't want to be a bother.

Though he couldn't see the ladder, he knew about where it was and lay down on his stomach near the spot. Scooting himself to the edge, he dangled his legs over the side of the roof, searching for the ladder with his feet.

Next thing he knew, he was sliding off. Shingles acted like sandpaper, while the edge of the roof—which he tried to grab to stop his descent—acted like a saw blade, slicing his left hand open. Rick hit the pavement below. My daughter heard the fall and hollered for help.

> If one person falls, the other can reach out and help.
> But people who are alone when they fall are in real
> trouble. (Eccl. 4:10)

We rushed Rick to the nearest doctor where his hand, mercy me, required forty-six stitches. Thirteen of those stitches were internal!

According to the doctor, there was something to be thankful for in this ordeal. The cut should have sliced right through one of the major nerves in Rick's hand. When this nerve is severed, much sensation and use of that hand is diminished.

The doctor called every available nurse in to see what he deemed "miraculous." There was no flesh left above the nerve, on either side of the nerve, or for a good distance underneath the nerve, but the nerve was completely intact. This nerve ran across the middle of the gash, untouched, like a bridge over a valley gorge.

This doctor was shocked, Rick was grateful, and I was just trying not to pass out. Later I felt thankful. Thankful for God's provision. Thankful that my daughter was nearby to hear his fall. Thankful that I was home to drive him to an urgent care facility. And thankful for doctors and nurses who can look inside the human hand and not throw up at the sight of it!

The healing period took several weeks. During that time Rick couldn't get his hand wet, or do many things he normally does around the house. He had to rely on my help.

I'd frequently find Rick in the kitchen or the garage trying to do a two-handed task with his one available hand. Our conversations went like this:

"Honey, can I lend you a hand?"

"No, I got it."

After watching him fumble another minute, "Why don't you let me help you?"

"That's, OK. I'm good."

"You don't *look* like you're good."

"Well, I am."

After watching him strain some more, "Rick, you're not good. You've got forty-six stitches, your hand is in a sling, and you need two hands to get that done."

Sigh. Reluctantly, "OK. Help me."

Help—I Need Somebody

After weeks of repeating this scene, Rick got better at asking for and receiving help. His hand healed as well. Today you'd never know that fall occurred.

My Yahweh Sisters, how many times do we find ourselves hanging dangerously off the side of some problem or the edge of some sin … searching on our own for a way down? Meanwhile, there is a Sisterhood nearby equipped by God to help.

> Share each other's troubles and problems, and in
> this way obey the law of Christ. (Gal. 6:2)

When will we wise up? The Christian life is not a one-person task. We regularly need encouragement, instruction, and help from one another. We must stop our knee-jerk insistence that we're fine and start being the body of Christ. Start functioning together as a community. A big part of that means asking for and receiving help.

Dr. Gary Smalley writes:

> To stay healthy, you have to receive from others.
> You need the resources that God wants to give
> you as well as the help and assistance he wants
> to provide through others. You must open your
> heart to God and to others in order to receive
> what you need. To practice good self-care, you
> must learn to let the love of God and others
> penetrate. You must allow God's love to sink into
> your soul. You must receive.[1]

Let me ask, how well do you receive? Any better than you ask
for help?

God wrote Rick a note—a lifelong reminder on his hand—with
a scar that says, "Ask for help." Yahweh Sisters, I pray it doesn't take a
scar or a nasty fall for that message to penetrate our skin as well.

BIBLE STUDY

1. Moses received some unsought advice from Jethro, his father-
   in-law. Read Exodus 18:13–27. What was Jethro's advice,
   and why did he offer it?

Did Moses take his advice?

It isn't stated, but what is implied of God's opinion of Jethro's advice?

2. Does God delegate—meaning does He ask, assign, and trust others to carry out His plans and desires? What does that tell you about your need to ask, assign, and trust others?

3. Solomon had a lot to say about the importance of sharing life and partnering effectively with others. Read Ecclesiastes 4:7–8. What about this man's life does Solomon consider a waste—what does he have and not have, do and not do?

Have you known someone who works extra hard, often at the expense of relationships, without questioning if this is wise? What is your opinion a life lived this way?

4. Continue reading in Ecclesiastes 4:9–12. List several benefits offered for partnering with people rather than going it alone.

What trends in modern society tend to tear at our relationships? Look at your own life; how are you responding to this?

Paul writes in Galatians 6:2–5:

> By helping each other with your troubles, you truly obey the law of Christ. If anyone thinks he is important when he really is not, he is only fooling himself. Each person should judge his own actions and not compare himself with others. Then he can be proud for what he himself has done. Each person must be responsible for himself. (NCV)

Paul begins this passage saying to help each other and winds up saying each person should be responsible for himself. So which is it? The difference is in the word *troubles* in verse 2, where some translations say "burdens." A burden is a load we cannot *reasonably* carry alone. For example, it is my job, not my friends', to provide dinner for my family each night. However, if I am sick with the flu, a friend can be a real help in that time of trouble by bringing over a pot of soup.

Some people will try to get you to carry their daily tasks that are not true burdens. Others will resist asking for help no matter how great their troubles. A wise woman—indeed a good friend—is discerning in these matters.

6. I once read about a woman named Kay who, shortly after having a miscarriage, saw her friend Marge for the first time in several weeks. Marge pulled Kay into her arms and whispered, "I'm so sorry about …" Marge didn't finish, afraid to say the wrong thing. Kay let go after a moment, but her friend didn't. She kept holding her. Kay squeezed back, but Marge still didn't let go. So Kay didn't stop hugging her friend until Marge pulled away. She said later that Marge had shown her more than love for the moment—she'd shown she'd hang on longer than her friend would admit she needed her.

A despairing man should have the devotion
of his friends. (Job 6:14 NIV)

When have you "hung on" to someone in need? When have you been hung on to?

9

Turn the Beat Around

Revealing the Secret of Rest

Last night I heard a familiar song emanating from my daughter's bedroom: "We Go Together" from the *Grease* soundtrack. I knew it by heart as a young girl but hadn't heard the song in years.

As Alaina danced and clapped around her room to the song, I bopped to the beat in the kitchen—managing to sing most of the rapid, nonsensical lyrics with a big smile of remembrance: *rama lama lama ka dinga da ding de dong shoo-bop sha wadda wadda yippidy boom de boom.*

You've heard a catchy song and clapped your hands along to the beat. Beats give music its rhythmic pattern. They're also used to count time when playing a piece of music or dancing to it.

Rests in a piece of music are the intervals of silence. They're the pauses between the beats. Without rests, there is little melody to the sounds. Without rests, we have but a long continuous noise, not unlike the jarring buzz of an alarm clock. That's an annoying sound to wake to, a difficult sound to dance to, and an impossible sound to live by.

Yet all too often I've tried.

Impatient Cow

A few years ago my daughter came to me with a joke:

"Knock-knock," she announced.

"Who's there?"

"Impatient cow."

"Impatient co ..."

"MOOOOO!" she interrupted me.

We both fell out laughing.

Yes, I am easily amused. I thought that was the funniest joke. However, I've come to realize that I am *such* the impatient cow. I can't or don't wait well. I interrupt because I'm anxious to say my part now. I want to speed up the process. I'm always looking to get to what I assume will be the good part.

It's a frenetic, self-centered mind-set.

One of my favorite writers, Canadian pastor Mark Buchanan, can relate. He reveals:

> Someone asked me recently what was my biggest regret in life. I thought a moment, surveying the vast and cluttered landscape of my blunders and losses, the evil I had done and the evil done to me.
>
> "Being in a hurry," I said.

"Pardon?"

"Being in a hurry. Getting to the next thing without fully entering the thing in front of me. I cannot think of a single advantage I've ever gained from being in a hurry. But a thousand broken and missed things, tens of thousands, lie in the wake of all that rushing."

Through all that haste, I thought I was making up time. It turns out I was throwing it away.[1]

Like Mark, I too have eroded precious, irreplaceable things in my effort to move forward or get more done. I've missed vital opportunities to teach my children or to leave a positive impression just by playing with them. I've missed chances to snuggle up with Rick on the couch and watch a movie because I was in the recliner with my laptop trying to answer email at the same time. I've missed passing the afternoon with a friend over a pot of tea or a walk on the beach. I've missed calling an aging relative to relive fond times, one last time.

I can't always remember exactly what I missed these moments for, but it sure seemed important at the time.

So Are the Days of Our Lives

Let me tell you how one of my Sundays went early in the year. I slept in. When I awoke, my husband was at our neighborhood gym working out and my kids were watching TV. Over breakfast, I looked through the newspaper. Then I opened my computer and noticed an email from an online store telling me I had three weeks to redeem

eight dollars in free merchandise credit. I surfed the store's site looking for the just right thing to buy before getting ready for church.

As we headed to the driveway, I suggested to Rick that we take two
cars to church so I could run some errands and do some shopping after
the service. After church, we went out to eat before Rick and the kids
went home and I went to four stores and a car dealership. Oh, and I
stopped by the grocery store too on the way home to grab a few things,
even though I already had dinner ready in the crock pot.

I arrived home to my husband on his laptop and my kids playing
outside with friends. I took my time unloading groceries, then sat
down to research a few things online, including one of the cars I had
looked at. After dark we had dinner together, and Rick read with the
kids before they went to bed. Meanwhile, I took down the last of the
Christmas decorations.

It was then that I remembered I needed to prepare my blog post
for the next morning. It was also then that the irony of my day hit
me full force, right between the eyes.

A few years ago, at a book convention, I met author Keri Wyatt
Kent. She had written a book called *Breathe: Creating Space for God
in a Hectic Life*. Don't you love that title? One of the main things
I learned from her was the importance of setting aside a day for
Sabbath-style rest and relaxation—making it a day to connect with
God and loved ones.

So I decided back in 2005 to become more intentional about
resting and connecting with God and family regularly each week.
We enjoyed the results. However, over time my commitment to
Sabbath rest eroded. Worse, I had barely noticed it until that
Sunday night scrambling to write my blog post.

I'd agreed before Christmas to interview Keri on my blog that Monday in January about her follow-up book on Sabbath-keeping called *Rest*. So naturally I panicked, then spent the remainder of my Sunday hurrying to post something profound about Sabbath rest. You see the irony too, don't you?

It's not that my day was hectic that Sunday. It's not like I skipped church to shop—wouldn't dream of it. Nor did I neglect or fight with my family. Plus, we shared two good meals together. But we didn't really connect, not deeply—not Sabbath style. Nor did I connect with God much beyond the public worship service. I certainly didn't rest. Overall, I'd say I spent the day more as an economic consumer than as a wife, mother, or child of God.

I went to bed that night heavy with this realization. After lying awake awhile, I climbed back out of bed, got on my knees in the dark, and asked God to help me make changes.

What's Different?

I asked visitors to my blog that week to tell me what their Sabbath days look like. Kim admitted, "Sunday seems to be like any other day except everyone is off from work." I'm guessing that's true for many of us. Our Sabbaths only differ in that we're off from school or work and we may attend church in addition to our usual activities. So Sundays look and sound the same, only we squeeze in one more thing—church.

God, however, intended for the Sabbath day to have an entirely different look, a different rhythm from the other days in our week. The weekly beat that God set our lives to rhythm with is *work—work—work—work—work—work—rest*. Repeat.

It's also the beat He lived as an example in the creation account in Genesis. If you are emotionally allergic to the word *work*, substitute the word *create* in that pattern. We create a home, we create order, we create income, we create business, we create meals—all this is our daily work.

How often do we create rest in this life song we've been given?

Most of us, if we're honest about it, live by the weekly rhythm *work—work—work—work—work—work—work*. Repeat, then collapse. (Oh, we may squeeze some TV watching or window shopping in there and call that rest.)

It's a frenetic, self-centered mind-set.

If this is not the rhythm God clapped out when establishing our breath song, are we out of rhythm with God and His purposes? What if what we're frantically seeking in the next thing can be found only in the rests with Him between the beats?

When I neglect rest I create disconnection in my relationships instead of connection. I create unrealistic expectations rather than a sense of accomplishment. I create disappointment and irritability rather than satisfaction and peace. And I create burnout and stress rather than energy and joy. Sometimes I even create insomnia, even though I am exhausted. Clearly I'm out of rhythm when this happens.

Check yourself here. When asked, "How have you been lately?" by friends or loved ones, what's your typical answer? I find "busy" replacing "fine" as the standard, accepted response.

We wear our busyness like a badge of honor, a signal of productivity and worth. We also use it as an excuse—even an excuse for not connecting with God. Remember the folks on the guest list in Jesus' parable who were too busy to come to the banquet on party day (Luke 14:15–24)?

Rest As Worship

In the fourth of the Ten Commandments, God instructed His people to spend one day each week resting from their work:

> "Remember to observe the Sabbath day by keeping it
> holy. Six days a week are set apart for your daily duties
> and regular work, but the seventh day is a day of rest
> dedicated to the LORD your God." (Ex. 20:8–10)

Looking at this passage it's easy to focus on the "rule part" that says we have six days to do stuff, and then we're suppose to rest. It's even easier to miss the "why part" that reveals this is necessary not only to relax our body and mind but also to worship God.

We know our body and mind need rest. When we push past that point, we get sick, cranky, and have trouble thinking clearly. We make mistakes. We fail tests. We yell at loved ones. We fall asleep behind the desk, TV, or wheel.

What we don't often realize is that stopping to rest is also an act of worship. It's not just something we do for ourselves—something we get to decide if and when it is needed. It's something we do with God, honoring Him.

You Bet Your Bottom Dollar

Rest is an act of trust. We lay our work aside and our head on the pillow, closing our eyes, trusting that we will wake again. Like freckle-faced Annies, we trust the sun will come out tomorrow.

We assume the earth will continue spinning and tilting at just the right degree to keep us all here. We trust the part where it says,

"He existed before everything else began, and he holds all creation together" (Col. 1:17).

Trust equals rest. King David knew this equation. If any man should have had trouble falling asleep, it would have been David. David was a man after God's own heart, but he was also a man with many enemies. His own son Absalom rebelled against him and gathered some ten thousand soldiers to kill him. So David left his palace and went on the run.

Out in the wilderness he had only trees or caves for cover. Only rocks for pillows. But each night he'd lie down and sleep like a baby. This is the man who penned Psalm 3:5: "I lie down and sleep; I wake again, because the LORD sustains me" (NIV). And Psalm 4:8 (NIV), "I will lie down and sleep in peace, for you alone, O LORD, make me dwell in safety."

No wonder God called David a man after His own heart. David learned that our ability to rest is directly and proportionally tied to our level of trust in God.

In fact, they go together like *rama lama lama ka dinga da ding de dong*. Remembered forever like *shoo-bop sha wadda wadda yippidy boom de boom*. Told you all those lyrics came flooding back last night.

It's not likely you and I will ever be on the run from tens of thousands of soldiers seeking to take our life, but it is likely that this very day we are pursued by compulsive busyness or chronic stress. It's imperative that you and I learn how to trust God and rest well.

Start Spreading the News

When done well, rest is more than trusting God with our breath or with the world in our temporary absence. True, that is a daring act of faith. But then again, we have no control over those things even while awake or working.

When done well, rest is a conscious act of worship and a means of holy transformation. Setting aside time to rest is setting aside time to become set apart. When we focus on Him in our rest, we become realigned with His heartbeat. We become *rest*ored to His image. Dedicating our rest, focusing it heavenward, turns it transcendent.

God is God—He's extraordinary! Why would His people need to be told to pause for a day in order to focus on Him? I agree— it's astonishingly necessary. If we don't stake out time to lean into God and look into His face, it's just not likely to happen. Hard to believe, yet totally true. And since that was true in the slower pace of ancient civilization when God gave this command, it's certainly true today.

The city that never sleeps is at least taking naps now. MetroNaps, an international company in conjunction with research from Carnegie Mellon University, created a way for exhausted employees, shop-till-you-droppers, and tired travelers to press pause. For four- teen dollars the weary can nap for twenty minutes in state-of-the-art sleep-pods in the Empire State Building.

If the sleep-pods didn't cost eight thousand dollars and look like EVE from the movie WALL-E, I'd consider buying one of these pods myself. (Right after I bought the expensive massaging chair from Brookstone.) Sleep-pods, however, don't match my decor.

New Yorkers now give each other the gift of rest with "nap passes" to the pods. What do you buy for stressed-out friends, fam- ily, or colleagues? What do you get the person who has everything? A break from it all of course—the metro nap.

Interesting concept. Problem is it takes more than an occasional nap—with or without a shiny, white sleep-pod—to produce the kind of rest our souls need. A catnap may cure physical fatigue, but it can't treat a disconnected heart. Your soul and mine literally *need* to worship God and connect meaningfully with Him. We must breathe God's restorative breath into our innermost being. Without pausing regularly to do that, we fall out of rhythm.

Lord of the Sabbath

I find it curious that God doesn't just tell His people to take a rest in the fourth commandment; He tells them to *remember* to take this rest. He knows how strong the pull is to keep going, keep doing, keep buying, keep creating, keep indulging, keep accomplishing, and forget to stop. He knows our tendency is to pause for a twenty-minute power nap once exhausted and then keep at it.

He knows without God-focused rest we become frenetic and self-centered.

A lot of debate surrounds Sabbath-keeping these days: What day does it have to be? Does it have to be a whole day? What exactly can you do and not do? Doesn't the new covenant in Christ free us from having to observe Old Testament Sabbath laws?

I'm not a theologian, so I avoid such debates. Here's what I know: I am to follow Jesus. Straight up, I'm a Jesus girl. When in doubt, I look to Him. Looking at Jesus' life in the Gospels, I see Him regularly working—preaching, healing, and mentoring. I also see Him regularly resting—escaping off to remote places to rest, recuperate, and connect with God or His disciples. Jesus told His followers to do the same.

As a Christian, I can get trapped by the feeling that there is so much important work to be done. There are people hurting who need encouragement. There are people wandering who need direction. There are people dying who need eternal life. How can I play checkers with my family when there are hungry people to feed? How can I sit and do yet another Bible study when there are souls out there to save? How can I lie down and sleep when there are citizens to serve?

When I start feeling this way—about ministry work or any other kind of work—I've lost sight of who is Lord of the Sabbath. It's Jesus. If He rested from His world-altering work, so can I.

So should I.

So must I.

Shake, Rattle, and Roll

In Mark 6, Jesus sends out His disciples in pairs to travel and work in the region without Him. It was their first big solo ministry tour. They cast out demons, healed the sick, taught many, and anointed people with oil. Can you imagine how excited they must have been to return to Jesus and tell Him about it?

When I imagine myself in their dusty sandals walking the road back to Jesus, I'm mentally rehearsing which stories I'd relay to Him. I'm hoping to light up His eyes with my tales of triumph in His name. I'd be ready to hear Him say, "Well done, Rachel. Now let's celebrate this successful venture. Bring out the harps, prepare the fireworks, let's dance and sing and throw a party! And we'll start planning the next tour."

Look at what Jesus actually said to them: "'Let's get away from the crowds for a while and rest.' There were so many people coming and going that Jesus and his apostles didn't even have time to eat. They left by boat for a quieter spot" (Mark 6:31–32).

What? No rockin' 'round-the-clock party? Surely they had enough adrenalin flowing to paint the village red. Yet resting is what Jesus was interested in. Quiet, reflective, restorative rest.

Rest and a satisfying meal together—that was the next thing on Jesus' agenda for them. Could it be the next thing on Jesus' agenda for you and me as well?

A New Song

Jesus, Lord of the Sabbath, is calling us to awaken to a new song. "Come to Me" is the chorus. "I will give you rest" is the refrain—"Come to me, all of you who are weary and carry heavy burdens, and I will give you rest. Take my yoke upon you. Let me teach you, because I am humble and gentle, and you will find rest for your souls" (Matt. 11:28–29).

Let's look at that invitation in *The Message:*

> "Are you tired? Worn out? Burned out on religion? Come to me. Get away with me and you'll recover your life. I'll show you how to take a real rest. Walk with me and work with me—watch how I do it. Learn the unforced rhythms of grace. I won't lay anything heavy or ill-fitting on you. Keep company with me and you'll learn to live freely and lightly."
> (vv. 28–30)

Jesus can help us take a real rest. He's willing to teach us how to rest well.

Marching to a Different Drum

In the modern, westernized world we tend to think of our days as sunup to sunup. In other words, we rise, we work, and then we end the day in rest. We rest to recover from our work … with whatever time is left over after the work is done.

However in the ancient Jewish tradition the day runs from sundown to sundown. That's a radically different concept. In other words, we rest, *then* we rise and do our work. Rest becomes the fuel and motivation for the work rather than merely recovery from it.

A secular rhythm makes work primary. We go from work to vacation. In contrast, a sacred rhythm makes rest primary, moving us from a Sabbath connection into our vocation. The sacred rhythm is rest, rise, work rather than rise, work, rest. Let that difference sink in and sway the tempo of your heart.

Internalizing this truth is the basis for resting well. Eugene Peterson describes this rest-first rhythm, conceived by a gracious God who never sleeps:

> This Hebrew evening/morning sequence conditions us to the rhythms of grace. We go to sleep, and God begins his work. As we sleep he develops his covenant. We wake and are called to participate in God's creative action. We respond in faith, in work. But always grace is previous. Grace is primary. We wake into a world we didn't make, into a salvation we didn't earn. Evening: God begins, without our help, his creative day. Morning: God calls us to

enjoy and share and develop the work he initiated. Creation and covenant are sheer grace and there to greet us every morning.[2]

Unchained Melody

I like to shop just as much as the next gal. I'm pretty sure I've established that here. However, in retrospect, I can't believe I thought Sunday morning before church was the best time to redeem a mere eight dollars in store credit that I had three whole weeks to use. Or that Sunday afternoon after lunching with my family was the best time to look at cars by myself—the dealership wasn't even open to answer my questions. Even they take Sundays off!

My rhythm of life is more melodic since that night in January when I got out of bed to ask Jesus to help me change. I'm learning to rest well, to rest as worship, and to rest as fuel for my work rather than recovery from it. I'm learning to let rest transform me.

I hope I don't fall off the rest wagon again anytime soon. Sabbath-style rest is a secret that I intend to keep. But should I slip, the great thing about Jesus is He's always willing to offer grace and help us get our groove back.

BIBLE STUDY

1. Imagine it is late afternoon and a package arrives via FedEx on your doorstep. Would you bring it in, or would you let it sit on the porch a few days? You'd likely bring it in.

Once you brought it inside would you open it or just set it aside for a week or two to open later? Sure, you'd probably open it that day—we're usually excited about packages. We know they're not junk mail, and often they contain gifts.

Now imagine that once a week a white package arrives with God's return address—would you want to tear into it right away? A gift from God! God gives us such packages—such gifts in the form of daily and weekly rests. Are you leaving them unopened?

Read Psalm 127:2. Try reading it in several translations at BibleGateway.com. Then write out this verse as a reminder to yourself.

2. From the following verses, summarize why we can take a real rest.

Isaiah 30:15

Psalm 62:1

Psalm 46:10

3. If you are confused by the debates regarding Sabbath-keeping, take a minute to pray, and then read Romans 14. Clarify your beliefs in the space below.

10

Crave a Clear Conscience More than Clear Skin

Revealing the Secret Beauty of Confessing Sins

Most women dread turning forty. Not me; I can hardly wait. Actually, it's forty-four I really want to be. I've been yearning for forty-four since the day I read that 12 percent of women experience acne until they are forty-four years old. I've been "experiencing" acne since age ten, and I loathe it.

I've gone to great lengths in my battle against breakouts: washing with salicylic acid, toning with witch hazel, moisturizing with benzoyl peroxide, swallowing supplements, spot-treating with sulfur, making masks from crushed aspirin, as well as trying natural concoctions from my kitchen blender. For about a month several years ago, in the winter no less, I endured a nightly icing down of my face with ice cubes before applying a special gel kept cold in the fridge.

A dermatologist recommended this. It didn't work. I did catch cold, though.

You do realize these are the antics of a desperate woman, right? It's uber-frustrating to be fighting acne and fine lines at the same time.

Honestly, I can't believe I'm admitting this to any of you clear-skinned gals. But I spent decades working to hide my blemishes with high-necked sweaters, down-swept bangs, or copious amounts of cover-up. Some days my skin looked so inflamed I didn't leave the house. I stayed undercover, in hiding.

Under Cover

We all have our hang-ups and flaws, as well as a strong impulse to hide them. Sometimes we use turtlenecks, sometimes concealer, and sometimes lies. Any of these sound familiar to you?

> *"Sorry I'm late again, but traffic was bad."* In reality, I left the house fifteen minutes late, because I got in the shower late, because I woke up late, because I stayed up too late reading that novel.

> *"Oh, the check is in the mail—you should be getting it any day now."* Reality is it will be in the mail as soon as I hang up and go write it. That is, right after I check my balance to make sure the check won't bounce after yesterday's shopping spree.

> *"No, honey, this isn't a new outfit; I've had it awhile."* Truth is I snuck it in the house two Saturdays ago

while you mowed the backyard, but *technically* I
have had it for a while.

"Did you hear about Jennifer? Well you should know,
just so you can pray for her...." Actually, I think I'll
explode if I don't tell this shocking piece of gossip.

Yes, the impulse to look good on the outside while lying, justifying,
or masking our real motives is strong. Jesus could see it in the faces
of everyone He met. In Luke 12 a massive crowd assembled to hear
Him speak. He'd certainly stirred up some dust with His recent
teachings, offending the religious leaders who prided themselves
on being holy. Jesus saw a different story when He looked at these
Pharisees' faces.

As Jesus watched, a chaotic crowd, including Pharisees, gathered.
Jesus used the occasion to reveal another secret to His disciples—a
secret about people's secrets:

Meanwhile, the crowds grew until thousands were
milling about and crushing each other. Jesus turned
first to his disciples and warned them, "Beware
of the yeast of the Pharisees—beware of their
hypocrisy. The time is coming when everything will
be revealed; all that is secret will be made public.
Whatever you have said in the dark will be heard
in the light, and what you have whispered behind
closed doors will be shouted from the housetops for
all to hear!" (Luke 12:1–3)

Beware. It's a strong word, isn't it? Jesus used it twice in this moment as He warned against saying one thing and living another. I imagine His warning unsettled the disciples. It does me. According to Jesus, nothing I hide will stay hidden forever. My sin will be revealed for what it is. My motives exposed for what they are. There is a day coming when the state of my complexion will be inconsequential, as the state of my character is revealed for all to see.

On that day, the tissue-thin image of innocence we've created for ourselves with lies, excuses, denials and half-truths will provide no cover.

When I let that truth sink in, I realize acne is the least of my troubles.

But I'm a Good Person

In old movies, I can usually tell the good guys from the bad guys. The good guys wear white and want justice. The bad guys wear black and seek their own selfish gain. Some movies I've seen, however, surprise me at the end with who is really on which side. Jesus told a story like that in Luke 18:10–14.

Jesus tells of two men who went into the temple to pray. We learn that the first guy is a ministry worker, a Pharisee. He carefully followed God's laws and encouraged others to as well. We learn that the second guy does not work in the service of God, but rather for the government in a job widely known to be filled with corruption. These workers had a reputation for abusing the system and swindling the citizens for their own profit.

From Jesus' description of their jobs, I picture the first guy looking clean-cut, praying with sincerity in his voice, and maybe even wearing a white robe. The second man I picture as somewhat dirty and gruff, with dark, intimidating eyes. I imagine him going through the motions of prayer—for show, but not really meaning it.

Not only does Jesus tell us the two men's occupation, but He also reveals exactly what they prayed. The first guy prayed in a customary manner for rabbis, according to the Talmud. He gives thanks to God that he is set apart as a holy man, unlike the government employee on the other side of the room. He prayed, "God, I thank You that I am not like other people: swindlers, unjust, adulterers, or even like this tax collector. I fast twice a week; I pay tithes of all that I get" (Luke 18:11–12 NASB).

The other man, however, wouldn't even approach the altar. Jesus said he stood at a distance, refusing to lift his eyes to heaven to address God directly. This man wasn't going through the motions of prayer as I would imagine; he was feeling quite emotional. He beat his fist to his chest, very aware of his need for God as he begged, "God, be merciful to me, the sinner!" (v. 13 NASB). It was this man, Jesus reveals, and not the first, who left that temple right with God.

The ending of the story shocked Jesus' audience. God didn't justify the religious leader of the Jewish people who fasted and tithed, but instead the tax collector for the Roman government who'd stolen from God's people. Why? Because good actions are never enough to save our souls from the sins we commit. Notice the tax collector was the only one of the two who actually *asked* to be forgiven. Acknowledging his sin, he humbly requested God's mercy.

I Don't Want to Talk About It

Years ago I entered my kitchen to find my preschool son covered with brown and purple splotches. Pulling apart the two sides of his lunch sandwich, he'd finger-painted in the peanut butter and licked off the jelly. Looking at the telltale mess on his face I asked, "Caleb, what are you doing?" Knowing our house rules about playing with food, he answered, "I don't want to tell you."

I was hearing this line a lot from him lately. Though caught red-handed, when confronted with his crimes my young son would insist, "I don't want to tell you!" It wasn't that he was unaware of what he had done wrong. Nor did he plead innocent of the crime. He simply did not want to talk about it, much less request mercy.

I can relate to that.

Israel's infamous King David could too.

David carried the mantle of God's choice for Israel's king. He also carried the label of a man after God's own heart. He was clearly one of the good guys. But he wasn't without sin. He had trouble resisting his neighbor's wife, and he slept with her—even getting her pregnant. Rather than admit the mess he'd created, he attempted to hide it by having her husband killed. Then he married her. As a powerful king, David was able to arrange things so that he wouldn't have to talk about his sin. Yet he couldn't escape his conscience.

In Psalm 32:2–5 David reports:

> Yes, what joy for those whose record the LORD has cleared of sin, whose lives are lived in complete honesty! When I refused to confess my sin, I was weak and miserable, and I groaned all day long. Day and night your hand of discipline was heavy

on me. My strength evaporated like water in the summer heat. Finally, I confessed all my sins to you and stopped trying to hide them. I said to myself, "I will confess my rebellion to the LORD." And you forgave me! All my guilt is gone.

David discovered that confession can be liberating!

So I have to recognize my need to confess and then do it—not because my salvation continually depends on it, but because my spiritual complexion does. I wonder if the praying Pharisee in Jesus' story realized his spiritual complexion needed cleansing. I suspect he looked at his white robes and righteous actions and ignored the hidden sin of his prideful heart. I suspect we do that sometimes too.

We go to church weekly and read the Bible. We sing worship songs while taking a meal to the mom who just had a baby. We fill shoeboxes with Christmas toys for children in poverty or volunteer our time at vacation Bible school. We stay so busy doing noble things that we avoid examining our sinful thoughts and motives like pride or jealousy. We also ignore the bitterness, unforgiveness, or judgment lurking in the dark crannies of the chambers of our heart. We focus on the parts we and everyone can see—making those look shiny and good—but inside we are blemished.

That makes us like the bad guys of the New Testament: the Pharisees. You'd expect the religious leaders of Jesus' day to have great integrity. In many people's eyes they did, but Jesus saw what others could not. His eyes penetrated past their facade to the reality of their hearts. "You are like whitewashed tombs," He said to them. "Beautiful on the outside but filled on the inside with dead people's bones and all sorts of impurity. You try to look like upright people outwardly, but inside your hearts are filled with hypocrisy and lawlessness" (Matt. 23:27–28).

These Pharisees were vigilant about keeping up appearances but reckless about maintaining a clear conscience before God. They acted morally, but not for God's pleasure or glory. Their morality was more for their own image and ego. To them it provided status and a means to "keep God off their backs." Or so they thought until Jesus revealed otherwise.

Eugene Peterson phrases Jesus' words to the Pharisees in Matthew 23:28 (MSG) like this: "People look at you and think you're saints, but beneath the skin you're total frauds." And that is the danger in staring at our skin while ignoring our heart. We exfoliate the outside but not the inside. Jesus instructed them, "Scour the insides, and then the gleaming surface will mean something" (v. 26 MSG).

I used to read the Gospels and think Jesus acted loving toward everyone—hotheads, adulteresses, prostitutes—except the Pharisees. He verbally slammed them frequently. For good reason, of course. I certainly didn't blame Him or think He was wrong. Yet it surprised me given Jesus' insistence that He came to save us, not judge or condemn us. Then it hit me. Pointing out the true state of their hearts, in no uncertain terms, was the most loving thing Jesus could do for the image-conscious Pharisees. Without recognition of their sin, they'd never see their need to repent.

How We Exfoliate

Our complexion can grow dull due to accumulating dead skin cells on the surface of our face. It becomes dry or flaky and needs scrubbing to reveal the fresh, healthy cells underneath. Likewise, the complexion of our heart can grow dull with dead "sin cells." How do we exfoliate the heart, scour the insides? "The waters of baptism do that for you, not by washing away dirt from your skin but by presenting you through Jesus' resurrection before God with a clear conscience" (1 Peter 3:21 MSG).

Acknowledging our sin before Him is key: "If we say we have no sin, we are only fooling ourselves and refusing to accept the truth. But if we confess our sins to him, he is faithful and just to forgive us and to cleanse us from every wrong" (1 John 1:8–9).

The impulse to hide our imperfections is powerful, but our longing to confess them to someone without being condemned is even stronger. In January 2005 a website called PostSecret.com launched with the purpose of publishing people's secrets, while allowing them to remain anonymous. Anyone can write a secret and mail it in on a postcard. Every Sunday, twenty new secrets are selected from the massive piles of submissions and published.

Entries range from admissions of sexual misconduct and criminal activity, to confessions of secret desires, embarrassing habits, or unfulfilled dreams. Some are shocking, some offensive, some silly, and many are sad. So many of us live with haunting secrets that keep us awake at night, destroying our spiritual vitality.

Whatever the secret, we have an innate need to unload it and become free of its captive power. I imagine a degree of relief lies in the notion I can confess something on a postcard to strangers, with no chance of repercussion. However, that has about as much power to deliver me from my secret's grip as motor oil has to cleanse my face. Nothing can truly rinse away the grime of our fears, burdens, and sins except the blood of Jesus Christ.

Shame has a way of building up and clouding the complexion of our hearts. We become mired in the notion that who we are or what we've done is so bad that God can't or won't forgive us. There is nothing biblical about that belief—Yahweh delights in forgiving repentant sinners! We simply have to ask, with genuine sorrow for our sin and with faith that He will cleanse it. Hebrews 10:22 says, "Let us go right into the presence of God, with true hearts fully trusting him. For our evil consciences have been sprinkled with Christ's blood to make us clean, and our bodies have been washed with pure water."

God doesn't want us to live feeling guilty and shameful about our past, our sins, or our screwups. Perpetually feeling bad about yourself produces nothing positive and keeps you focused on self.

Rather, God wants us to see how we have betrayed Him, seek forgiveness, and be cleansed. Then we turn away from our sin by changing the way we operate. As John told the people who were seeking baptism either to purge themselves of guilt or because it was the "in" thing to do, "It's your life that must change, not your skin" (Luke 3:8 MSG). We must remember that what we say and do in secret will eventually come into the light—so our lives must change.

Here's the deal, girls. When Jesus said, "I have not come to call the righteous, but sinners to repentance" (Luke 5:32 NIV), Jesus wasn't implying that some gals are so good they don't need mercy. He meant that some gals assume they are. When we are honest with

God about our struggles with sin, we receive more than enough grace to cover them. That means we can stop pretending to hide them from Him, others, and ourselves. We can drop the concealer and the turtlenecks. We can toss back our hair, come out of hiding, and connect fully again. No postcards required.

And when we turn from sin and live according to God's commands—keeping His secrets rather than our own—not only are we cleansed, but we begin to glow with spiritual health. We become luminous, God's fresh-faced cover girl. We shine like a city on a hill at night. This is God's desire for us and He'll help us achieve it. Psalm 34:5 (NIV) assures, "Those who look to him are radiant; their faces are never covered with shame."

Embracing My Skin, Rejecting My Sin

I named my daughter *Alaina,* which means "bright, shining light." It's my hope that she will radiate the stunning image of God as she learns to embrace her own skin and reject her own tendency to sin. In fact, I pray this for her every time I tuck her into bed.

As I sit at her bedside, pulling her duvet up to her chin, she studies my complexion. At least once a month she comments that she can see my pores, and that they're big. *Great—as if I didn't spend enough time worrying about my clogged pores, now my daughter informs me they are also huge. How did I not notice this all these years of staring into my 5x magnification mirror?*

A couple nights ago as I was tucking Alaina in by the light of her bedside reading lamp she reached up her fifth-grade arms, pulled back my hair from my face, and looked at me intently. She announced, "I can see your pores."

"Yes, I'm aware you can," I replied. What I try to cover with powder becomes all too evident in the direct beam of a sixty-watt bulb.

"And your skin is all shiny, like it's oily."

"Is it?" I ask trying not to sound too annoyed.

Suddenly I realize it's been twenty years since I've seen my own mother's face. I can still picture her. I see her brown smiling eyes. I see the fine, downy blond hair that gently covered the sides of her cheeks. It wasn't perceptible when she had make-up on, or in dim light. But I remember noticing it in the morning sunlight when she walked about the house in her satin green robe, drinking coffee before work. I see the details of her face in my mind's eye, imperfections and all. The image warms me.

Then I flash forward in time. It occurs to me that when I'm gone, Alaina will close her eyes and picture me right like this ... leaning over her bedside, praying for her, telling her how much I love her—with my big pores, blemishes, and all. And the image will comfort her. The spirit of love will flow through her memory, despite my clogged pores.

"You are beautiful, Mommy." Her precious voice interrupts my thoughts, pulling me into the present. Then she adds, "I love your face—you have pretty skin." Turns out she likes my big, shiny pores.

After tucking her in, I smile and head to my bathroom to study this face she deemed beautiful. I see a pimple, and a few lines, and a faint but noticeable spot on my cheek the sun has darkened. I pause and make a pact with myself. Each time I gaze into my round, magnifying cosmetics mirror to examine a blemish or pluck a stray eyebrow, I will let it remind me to examine my heart for blemishes as well.

I will take those opportunities to pluck from my soul any unconfessed sin and ask God to rinse it away beneath the ongoing flow of His great grace. I'll use my propensity to stare at my surface to remind me to scour my heart.

Age forty-four looms out on my horizon. Maybe my skin will change by then. Perhaps it will look as good by the light of my daughter's lamp as it does in her clearly biased estimation. But I'm doubtful.

"The time is coming when everything will be revealed; all that is secret will be made public," Jesus warned (Luke 12:2). This day is also sitting somewhere on my horizon, and on yours. When that reality sinks in, what I really crave isn't clear skin but a clear conscience before God. I don't want to change my skin as much as I want to change my life by noticing my motives and rejecting my sin. Jesus reminds us, "You are masters at making yourselves look good in front of others, but God knows what's behind the appearance" (Luke 16:15 MSG).

My prayer is that you'll take this challenge too. That when you stand before your bathroom mirror this evening, washing off the remains of the day, you'll remember to exfoliate the inside. That you'll ask the Holy Spirit to search your heart and show you any spot that needs treating with Christ's blood, and that you'll confess.

May our beauty rituals include preventing neither sin nor shame to build up between our hearts and Yahweh's. For then our faces will shine with the brightness of His, no matter our age or the condition of our pores. Of that I am certain!

BIBLE STUDY

1. I mentioned David's bout with unconfessed sin. David wrote
   Psalm 51 after his affair with Bathsheba, and after Nathan
   forced him to finally confront what he'd done. Let's look at
   David's words:

   > Generous in love—God, give grace! Huge in
   >   mercy—wipe out my bad record.
   > Scrub away my guilt,
   >   soak out my sins in your laundry.
   > I know how bad I've been; my sins are staring me
   >   down. (Ps. 51:1–3 MSG)

   David begins this psalm by revealing something about himself and something about God. What are those things?

   This is what the Pharisees, with all their Bible knowledge and
   good deeds, were missing!

2. David continues in Psalm 51:

   > You're the One I've violated, and you've seen it all,
   >   seen the full extent of my evil.

You have all the facts before you;
   whatever you decide about me is fair.
I've been out of step with you for a long time,
   in the wrong since before I was born.
   (vv. 4–5 MSG)

Look at the reality David points out in verse 5—that we all wrestle a tendency to sin. It may be a tendency toward glaring sins like adultery or tax fraud, or toward almost unperceivable sins like haughtiness or an attitude of entitlement. Let's read on:

What you're after is truth from the inside out.
   Enter me, then; conceive a new, true life.
Soak me in your laundry and I'll come out clean,
   scrub me and I'll have a snow-white life.
Tune me in to foot-tapping songs,
   set these once-broken bones to dancing.
Don't look too close for blemishes,
   give me a clean bill of health. (vv. 6–9 MSG)

What I eat, what I allow on the inside, can impact how my skin looks outwardly. David tells us in verse 6 that true life—truthful life—comes from the inside out as well. How does that happen, according to this passage?

Who does the scrubbing, you or God? Explain.

3. To me, reading Psalm 32 is like watching a trained dancer leap and soar across the stage. It's like a ballet set to words. Take out your Bible and read it. David wrote this after he wrote Psalm 51, after God had washed clean the complexion of his heart. Sometimes we avoid confessing because we fear condemnation, distance, or punishment from God. So we ignore our guilt, hoping both we and God will soon forget it. What does David say resulted from his confession? List at least three outcomes of confession according to Psalm 32.

4. As Yahweh Sisters, confession is not about maintaining our salvation. If I were to perish without confessing my latest sin, I am not going to face eternal damnation. For believers, confession is about our spiritual vitality and our quality of life on *this* side of eternity.

Read 1 Timothy 1:18–20. What is the danger in not keeping a clear conscience?

Now look up 1 John 3:21–22. What are the fabulous benefits of keeping a clear heart before God?

5. Read Mark 1:1–15 about the start of Jesus' public ministry. What is the very first command Jesus issued, found in
   verse 15?

   Spiritual vitality also begins with this verb.

6. What has experience taught you about confessing your sins?
   Try your hand, like David, at writing a psalm about it.

11

Diversify your Portfolio

Revealing the Secret of True Security

For the record, I put no stock whatsoever in fortune cookies. Or horoscopes, or mood rings, or anything else of the sort. I do, however, like eating fortune cookies and in the process I usually read the tiny slip of paper inside. My husband and I get a kick out of these so-called fortunes. As a writer, I've often wondered what life is like for the fortune-cookie writer. I think I could finish work in twenty minutes a day!

My husband always winds up with the lamest cookie-fortunes. He gets messages like: "You are part way there." Or, "Another day is coming." Or else he gets vague ones like: "You will soon be more aware of your growing awareness." Mostly, he gets ones that seem lost in translation: "You may love the small ones but win the big ones." Or, "Your life is not a struggle. It's a wiggle." No real wisdom there. Yes, Rick was the king of senseless cookie-fortunes, until last weekend.

On Saturday Rick got what some fortune writer probably thought was the ultimate. It said, "You have inexhaustible wisdom and power." Rick dramatically read it aloud to me with a smile and awaited my response: "Wow, Honey. Evidently you're God!" Rick pumped his fist in the air and exclaimed, "YESSS! I *knew* it!" We laughed until tears soaked our sesame chicken.

The rest of the weekend, every time I'd ask Rick a question—like what time it is—he would answer and then add, "There's more where that came from, because I have inexhaustible wisdom!" When asked to open the spaghetti sauce jar he said, "Sure, because I have inexhaustible power!" Isn't it ridiculous to think any human possesses inexhaustible wisdom and power? Rick is wonderful, but Superman he is not.

It's entirely accurate, however, to say that Rick has *access* to inexhaustible wisdom and power. So do you and I as Sisters in Christ. Catch this: "To those called by God to salvation, both Jews and Gentiles, Christ is the mighty power of God and the wonderful wisdom of God" (1 Cor. 1:24). As Christ followers, we have all-access passes to inexhaustible wisdom and power!

Staking It All

Daniel was considered a wise man—in fact, among the wisest in the ancient nation of Babylon. He'd been taken to Babylon by King Nebuchadnezzar's court chief, following Israel's loss to the Babylonians. Daniel was forced to serve their king as a teacher and adviser, as part of a group of magicians, astrologers, and enchanters the king relied on to make decisions and predictions. I reckon fortune cookies weren't invented yet.

Daniel did his best to keep himself pure before God under these circumstances. The Bible says that because of this, God gave him "an unusual aptitude for learning the literature and science of the time. And God gave Daniel special ability in understanding the meanings of visions and dreams" (Dan. 1:17). It also says that in all matters requiring wisdom and judgment, the king found Daniel's advice to be "ten times better than that of all the magicians and enchanters in his entire kingdom" (v. 20).

One night King Nebuchadnezzar had a nightmare. When none of the astrologers, magicians, and enchanters could interpret his dream, he sent an angry decree for all his royal advisers to be killed. Daniel learned of this and sought God for wisdom to interpret the dream. God granted it, sparing Daniel's life and the rest of the Babylonian wise men.

Read carefully Daniel's response to God's gracious provision:

> "Praise the name of God forever and ever, for he alone has all wisdom and power. He determines the course of world events; he removes kings and sets others on the throne. He gives wisdom to the wise and knowledge to the scholars. He reveals deep and mysterious things and knows what lies hidden in darkness, though he himself is surrounded by light. I thank and praise you, God of my ancestors, for you have given me wisdom and strength." (Dan. 2:20–23)

After Daniel explained the meaning of the dream and the fact that both the dream and its interpretation were provided by God,

King Nebuchadnezzar bowed before Daniel and honored him—
and his God. He lavished Daniel with gifts. He promoted Daniel
to head of his advisers and made him a ruler over the providence
of Babylon.

Daniel staked his life and security on his access to God's wisdom.
And it secured him. Mind if I ask what you tend to stake your security and future on?

The Almighty Dollar

Many people stake their security and future on money. It's certainly
been drilled into my middle-class head to secure my future with
money … get a good paying job, pay into Social Security, contribute
to a retirement account, and invest in stocks and mutual funds.

I left college with that plan in mind and promptly got a job as
a church-based preschool teacher. Noble perhaps, but not exactly
lucrative. After that I went to work for a mortgage corporation.
While I knew how to process the loans and what to say to custom-
ers on the phone, I didn't understand half the financial terms I was
throwing around. My next couple jobs were with universities, the last
of which provided a retirement account and a financial adviser for it.
Finally, someone would help me use my money to secure my future.

Bursting Bubbles

One icy winter afternoon in 2000, Rick and I sat at our kitchen table
talking with the financial adviser. You should know that Rick is fairly
conservative when it comes to certain things. He likes to play it safe
with fashion, roller coasters, heights, and money. I am more of a risk
taker in all of these areas.

Our adviser said the hottest thing to invest in at the moment—the stocks *sure* to make us money right now—were "tech stocks." Around this time, market investors were in a frenzy over what seemed the limitless potential of the Internet as a cash cow for companies daring enough to operate entirely online.

After hearing the adviser out, Rick agreed to invest a little bit in technology stocks, but he wanted to invest the majority of our retirement savings in more conservative ways. I didn't understand why Rick didn't want to make lots of money with tech stocks. I was ready to go all in!

I confess, I began chiding Rick about his conservative nature. Yours truly did not respect her husband's wishes on this one. The adviser was on my side, and Rick caved a bit to our joint pressure, agreeing to put roughly half our investment money into tech stocks.

Within a few months, the tech-stock bubble burst. We had staked so much of our financial portfolio on this one category of stock that when it plummeted, so did our portfolio's value. I've since learned the beauty of diversifying my investments, so that when one sector fails, others still hold value. In other words, don't put all nest eggs into one basket. Oh, and I also learned not to pressure Rick into financial decisions.

Like that dot-com crash or the more recent sub-prime housing market collapse, money-based sources of security are inherently risky. Their values can and will rise and fall. You and I need something more solid to count on for our security.

We need something less temporary and fallible to secure us. We need to tie our future to something unaffected by interest rates, rulers, the stock index, terrorist attacks, greed, or human error. We, like Daniel, need access to the basket of God's eternal wisdom.

Skipping Rocks

I'm not implying saving or investing is a bad idea—not at all—but it should not be our only means of security. It is not a sure thing. The truth is, we don't even have enough bars of silver and gold to back the amount of dollars in circulation today.

As much as I love bling, it can't safeguard me. Gold, silver, diamonds, land, jewels—all will fail as sources of security. There is no type of rock on which to secure our future except the solid rock of Jesus Christ. He is the Rock of Ages, the Cornerstone upon which our Sisterhood is built. He is both our foundation and our storehouse of treasure: "He will be your sure foundation, providing a rich store of salvation, wisdom, and knowledge. The fear of the LORD is the key to this treasure" (Isa. 33:6).

The treasures of God, the deep mysteries and wisdom of God, are encapsulated in this rock called Christ—contained in who He is, in what He did while here, in what He does now while risen, and in what He will do in the future when He returns. No gold-beaded necklace comes close to that.

Skipping Beads

One weekend I spoke at a women's retreat put on by a group of thoughtful ladies. When we broke for lunch, we entered a room with beautifully decorated tables. Each place setting had a shiny gold bookmark to take home as a gift. The bookmarks had different colored beads and Scripture verses attached.

I chose a table toward the back of the room and sat down. The gals already seated were trading bookmarks based on which color beads they liked best.

The kind sister next to me offered me her bookmark—"Rachel, these beads are your colors; they match your outfit." I thanked her for the offer but told her I would stick with the one at my seat. Though the brown beads on my bookmark were lackluster compared to the colored ones she offered, the verse on mine read, "Call to me and I will answer you and tell you great and unsearchable things you do not know" (Jer. 33:3 NIV). The promise of that verse is about the only thing that could cause me to pass on shiny bling!

Got Wisdom?

What is wisdom? Where do we find it? Is it different from the knowledge we learned in school? Since becoming a Christ follower, I've desired to understand the things of God and the ways of God. I've searched for and prayed for His wisdom. I wouldn't dare say I've fully attained it, but I've grown in wisdom for sure.

Wisdom is the ability to discern right from wrong, to understand what is true and lasting, and to skillfully act based on this information. In the book of Proverbs, wisdom is personified as a woman. She calls out in the streets for people to follow her (1:20–21). In the Gospels, wisdom is fully personified in the person and life of Jesus Christ. He hangs on a cross, then rises from the dead to ascend into heaven, inviting us to follow Him. Paul plainly tells us that Christ *is* the wisdom of God (1 Cor. 1:24).

"Fear of the LORD" is the starting point for wisdom (Prov. 1:7). This doesn't mean being afraid of God, who lovingly offers mercy through

Christ, but fearing His judgment, which we deserve apart from Christ. Hence, Wisdom's first call is a call to salvation (vv. 20–33).

What exactly does fearing the Lord entail? Respecting Him. And it will lead to wisdom: "The LORD tells his secrets to those who respect him" (Psalm 25:14 NCV).

Girls, if you are going to make only one investment this year—get wisdom! Wisdom tells us what she is worth and describes what it looks like to fear the Lord:

> Choose my instruction rather than silver, and knowledge rather than pure gold. For wisdom is far more valuable than rubies. Nothing you desire can compare with it.
>
> I, Wisdom, live together with good judgment. I know where to discover knowledge and discernment. All who fear the LORD will hate evil. That is why I hate pride, arrogance, corruption, and perverted speech. (Prov. 8:10–13)

She goes on to promise tremendous gain—greater than E. F. Hutton, E*Trade, or Merrill Lynch can provide—for those who follow her ways:

> Good advice and success belong to me. Insight and strength are mine. Because of me, kings reign, and rulers make just laws. Rulers lead with my help, and nobles make righteous judgments.

I love all who love me. Those who search for me will surely find me. Unending riches, honor, wealth, and justice are mine to distribute. My gifts are better than the purest gold, my wages better than sterling silver! I walk in righteousness, in paths of justice. Those who love me inherit wealth, for I fill their treasuries. (Prov. 8:14–21)

Insight, strength, riches, honor, wealth, and justice are Wisdom's to distribute. (And remember, Paul taught that Christ *is* wisdom.) And they are unending, inexhaustible. Wisdom's promise is that she and her great treasury will be found by those who seek her.

To seek is to find in God's kingdom. To know Christ, pray in His name, and obey His commands is to have access to all the wisdom, power, and wealth of heaven. To imitate Christ is to follow Wisdom's path. Sadly, my teachers never taught me this in school—yet it is the thing we all need to know.

For the Asking

While Christ *is* wisdom, and His life its ultimate example, King Solomon's life is another case study in wisdom and the security it brings. Solomon was born to King David nearly a thousand years before Christ. As a young lad—probably a tween or teen—he was installed as king before his father's death.

A short while after Solomon's ordination, God appeared to the young king in a dream and invited him to make any request. "God said, 'What do you want? Ask, and I will give it to you!'" (1 Kings 3:5).

Imagine your teenage self from years ago. Now imagine God—in almost genie-like fashion, though God is most certainly not a genie—asking you to make a request. What would you ask for?

After doing the happy dance at my good fortune to be asked by God to name a request, my teen self would have had trouble deciding on just one thing. I might've asked for a horse, a new wardrobe, a little sister, a sports car, a starring role in a Disney movie, to be rid of my rival Jolene, or maybe for a date with singer Shawn Cassidy.

Young Solomon had something entirely different in mind. He replied:

> "Now, O LORD my God, now you have made me king instead of my father, David, but I am like a little child who doesn't know his way around. And here I am among your own chosen people, a nation so great they are too numerous to count! Give me an understanding mind so that I can govern your people well and know the difference between right and wrong. For who by himself is able to govern this great nation of yours?" (1 Kings 3:7–9)

Good Choice!

Feeling the weight of his responsibilities, Solomon asked God for the thing he would need to fulfill his purpose in the future. He asked for something to enable him to lead the people and judge fairly among them. Approving of Solomon's request for wisdom, God answered:

"Because you have asked for wisdom in governing my people and have not asked for a long life or riches for yourself or the death of your enemies—I will give you what you asked for! I will give you a wise and understanding mind such as no one else has ever had or ever will have! And I will also give you what you did not ask for—riches and honor! No other king in all the world will be compared to you for the rest of your life! And if you follow me and obey my commands as your father, David, did, I will give you a long life." (1 Kings 3:11–14)

Talk about doing the happy dance—what an astonishing blessing. Did you notice all those exclamation points? Evidently God was *verrrrry* pleased to be asked for wisdom.

God granted Solomon wisdom, and as Solomon followed it, all God promised came true. In short order, Solomon's wealth grew tremendously. He owned property, livestock, and mines. He had twelve thousand horsemen on his payroll, managing his four thousand chariots. In today's market, he would be a multibillionaire or even a trillionaire.

Solomon's reputation was renowned. Kings from all over the world came to listen to and learn from him. Indeed Solomon still holds the title of the wisest man who ever lived (Jesus not included in a list of mere men).

Solomon's wisdom—flowing from the throne of God—brought the nation peace and prosperity like it had never known before. The forty years when Solomon sat as king were the best years in Israel's history. All because he asked God for wisdom and followed it.

What's in Your Wallet?

What is the most valuable thing on earth? It's not the Hope Diamond. It's not the National Treasury. It's not a Picasso collection, or the Microsoft fortune. It is the wisdom of God, seen in the pages of your Bible. You've had access to it all along.

Successful Yahweh Sisters diversify their portfolios with God's wisdom. Its value surpasses all else and compounds over time. It's the only sure foundation on which to stake our security and future.

Wisdom calls to us, urging us to make her our supreme investment. The Bible tells us to value wisdom more highly than we value our salaries or possessions: "Get wisdom—it's worth more than money; choose insight over income every time" (Prov. 16:16 MSG).

This is the plan I'm allowing Christ to drill into my head now: Savvy Yahweh Sisters make wisdom the predominant asset in their net worth. And how do we get this wisdom? Open the pages of your Bible and read. Regularly.

BIBLE STUDY

1. As mentioned, Daniel relied on God for wisdom in his dealings with King Nebuchadnezzar (detailed in Daniel 1 and 2), and it secured his life. Read Daniel 5 to see Daniel's later interaction with a subsequent Babylonian king, King Belshazzar.

   What foolishness plagued Nebuchadnezzar and later Belshazzar?

What was the outcome of the two kings' foolishness? And what was the outcome for Daniel, who clung to God's wisdom?

2. What if you're not really the intellectual type—you didn't go to Harvard or qualify to serve on the President's Cabinet. Do you have to be super smart in order to grasp God's wisdom? Read 1 Corinthians 1:24–29 and James 1:5 and answer this question.

3. Proverbs 3 shows us how the wisdom of God secures us. Read it and complete the chart below. Write the wise actions required on our part and the rewards they lead to.

Verses	Required Action	Reward
3:1–2		
3:3–4		
3:5–6		
3:7–8		
3:9–10		
3:13–18		
3:21–26		

4. Read James 3:13–18. List the attributes and outcomes of worldly "wisdom" and of godly wisdom from these verses.

    Worldly wisdom:

    Godly Wisdom:

5. As a means of investing in the wisdom of God and "diversifying your portfolio," begin reading one chapter from Proverbs each day. It takes only minutes, and there are enough chapters to provide a month's worth of readings.

12

Become a Recording Artist

Revealing the Secret of Disclosure

Secrets vary widely—from those worth keeping to those just too juicy to keep to yourself. The divine truths you've read between these pages fit into both of those categories.

At the time I discovered the truth of Jesus, I was twenty-one, attending college, and working in a bar. Within a year I'd led one patron, two fry cooks, two ex-boyfriends, and another waitress to our Lord. I had no idea how unusual that was.

I assumed every Christian shared her faith. I thought everyone talked about their Jesus and the amazing things He does in our hearts and lives. I couldn't imagine why we wouldn't.

Most of those people I introduced to Jesus never set foot in my church. They just saw the changes in me and heard the positive things I had to say about it. One by one they asked me to help them find that too.

I recall sitting at the wooden bar, cigarette smoke lingering in the air long after closing time, leading a young fry cook from a rough side of town in a prayer for forgiveness and salvation. But we talked for nearly an hour about Jesus and the Bible before he got to that point.

Knowing little about spiritual matters at the time, I answered his questions best I could (while praying under my breath for God's guidance). What I discovered is God draws people to Himself; that part isn't up to me. I'm just a guide on the path pointing the way to Him.

Afterward, I drove him home to an unsafe part of town, because he'd skipped his ride to stay and talk with me. I can still picture that middle-of-the-night full winter moon out my windshield. And the two of us cold and sleepy but elated, enamored with the invitation to be a part of God's eternal empire.

I imagined my life would be a series of events like this, casually introducing the people I knew to Christ. Months later, however, I moved across the state with my new husband to attend a Christian graduate school. Within weeks I took a job at the school. Suddenly I was surrounded by believers—at school and work and church. I lived in a sweet, sterile faith-bubble for the next several years.

While there I grew spiritually, but I nearly forgot how to talk to outsiders about Yahweh and His mysterious plan for abundant, eternal life. I learned His kingdom secrets and how to keep them, but I failed to share them with those outside the Sisterhood.

Whaddya Know?

Yahweh Sisters embody God's hidden wisdom for vibrant life. We know where to find forgiveness, deliverance, sound counsel, comfort, security, and restoration. Everyone needs this knowledge!

Most "rulers" of our age—the philosophers, statesmen, poets, celebrities, politicians, CEOs, self-help authors, professors, and talk-show hosts—know nothing of this secret knowledge because they're missing the decoder ring. While their advice may sometimes line up with the wisdom of God, it is often shortsighted or misleading. So you and I must speak up and share these secrets.

Paul made a point to speak to others with words of Yahweh's wisdom:

> But not the kind of wisdom that belongs to this world, and not the kind that appeals to the rulers of this world, who are being brought to nothing. No, the wisdom we speak of is the secret wisdom of God, which was hidden in former times, though he made it for our benefit before the world began. But the rulers of this world have not understood it; if they had, they would never have crucified our glorious Lord. That is what the Scriptures mean when they say,
>
> "No eye has seen, no ear has heard,
>   and no mind has imagined
> what God has prepared
>   for those who love him."
>
> But we know these things because God has revealed them to us by his Spirit, and his Spirit searches out

everything and shows us even God's deep secrets.
(1 Cor. 2:6–10)

These days, God reveals these things to us by His Spirit. We enjoy
the privilege—and benefit—of seeing and grasping secrets of the
kingdom of heaven while here on earth.

The secrets in this book by no means encompass the sum total
of God's deep secrets. But as we remember and apply these, Jesus
promises more understanding will be revealed to us (Matt. 13:12). In
this way God's kingdom is ever illuminated in this world.

God calls Yahweh girls to be His secret-keepers *and* His secret-
revealers. When we live His ways, we outline His image and trace
the truths of His kingdom before a watching world. Not only that,
but when we speak of Him to others, the kingdom grows. And God
takes pleasured notice:

> All those who truly respected the LORD and
> honored his name started discussing these things,
> and when God saw what was happening, he had
> their names written as a reminder in his book.
> (Mal. 3:16 CEV)

This verse reveals that Yahweh takes note when His girls talk about
Him. He deems this worthy of recording on His scroll of remembrance (NIV). The Author of life who pens your story observes each
time you discuss Him and honor His name before others! Aren't you
just a little curious how many times your name appears on that list?
I am.

A Star Is Born

Jesus tells the story of a woman from that list. I'm guessing her name was difficult for the townspeople of Sychar to remember because it kept changing. Married five times, she lived with yet another man when she met Jesus.

She had come to the well at the edge of her Samarian town to get water in the middle of the day. Most women avoided the heat of the day, preferring to draw water closer to dawn or dusk. It's curious she didn't follow suit. Perhaps she'd had a fight with her man and decided to get away alone awhile. Or perhaps she preferred avoiding the other women—her situation too embarrassing. Or maybe God had scheduled a divine appointment with her that day. Whatever the reason, on this day she came alone to the well in the blazing sun.

Also curious is the fact that Jesus, the young Jewish rabbi, was there alone waiting for His disciples to return with food from Sychar. At that time, Jews disliked Samaritans. In fact, they avoided Samarian towns, preferring to journey around rather than through them. Jewish rabbis wouldn't care to set foot among such pagans. And a rabbi certainly wouldn't speak to a foreign woman—that broke all the rules.

But Jesus did.

When the woman approached, He politely asked her to draw Him a drink of water. Again, most Jews would not drink from the same jug as this woman, for fear it would make them ritually unclean. Taken aback, she mustered the guts to question Him: "You are a Jew, and I am a Samaritan woman. Why are you asking me for a drink?" (John 4:9).

He rocked her world with His reply—"If you only knew the gift

God has for you and who I am, you would ask me, and I would give you living water" (v. 10).

His words took aim straight for the heart.

Contemplate His statement to her for just a minute.

What must her thought process have been? *If I only knew … what? What am I missing? A gift from God? For me? From whose God? What could it be? Am I speaking to someone significant here at this well? Who? How is there such a thing as water that lives?*

Her mind must've been reeling. *Is He some sort of prophet or poet? Maybe I should walk away. Maybe I should call His bluff. Maybe He's dehydrated and delusional.* She responded logically to Jesus, pointing out the fact that He didn't have anything to draw water with so He couldn't possibly give her water. She also noted that that particular well had historically good water—how could He offer her better water?

Jesus replied, "People soon become thirsty again after drinking this water. But the water I give them takes away thirst altogether. It becomes a perpetual spring within them, giving them eternal life" (vv. 13–14).

Intrigued, she responded, "Please, sir … give me that water! Then I'll never be thirsty again, and I won't have to come here to haul water" (v. 15). She's willing to believe Him but not fully tracking with His offer.

Jesus then referenced things about her that a stranger could not have known—such as her many past husbands. Convinced Jesus was a prophet, she asked Him about the differences between Jewish and Samaritan worship practices. In the course of their discussion Jesus reveals to her, "I am the Messiah!" (v. 26).

Not even His disciples had heard Him proclaim this yet. Plus, this sister's conversation with Jesus is the longest personal conversation with Christ recorded in the Bible. He really wanted her to realize the truth of who He was, to find her way into the Yahweh Sisterhood.

Get it, she did. She left her water jar beside the well and sprinted back to the village to shout, "Come and see a man who told me everything I ever did! Can this be the Messiah?" (v. 29). She had found living water at a common well on a blistering afternoon—like a treasure in a field, or a pearl of great price—and she urged others to behold it. Believing her claims, they came and begged Him to stay awhile among them.

For two days Jesus preached. Many Samaritans from the village listened and drank from the living water. Then they told the woman, "Now we believe because we have heard him ourselves, not just because of what you told us. He is indeed the Savior of the world" (v. 42).

Like me, she was thrilled to tell others about the Messiah she'd found. The Bible never reveals her name, but we can be sure God knows it and wrote it down. If we reviewed the entries for those days on His scroll of remembrance, I suspect we'd see her name bolded across the top of the page.

Her encounter with Jesus is one of the most remarkable, socially unacceptable, countercultural interactions in all of Scripture. "Discovered" by Jesus at a well, a Samaritan female found eternal life through the power of the Jewish Messiah. She stirred an overnight sensation with her words to the townspeople—resulting in a multitude of Gentile followers.

She simply pointed the way to Him.

When you understand fully who Jesus is, it awakens you. You just can't keep quiet about it. And "you shine like stars in the universe as you hold out the word of life" (Phil. 2:15–16 NIV).

The Samaritan woman at the well responded to Christ, becoming one of the original non-Hebrew Yahweh Sisters. Her name appears in the Book of Life and also on God's scroll of remembrance. How many times is your name or mine recorded on God's list of gals who talk about Him?

A better question is: How can we increase the number of times our name appears there? Zeal to tell others of Christ flows naturally when a woman becomes a believer. Let's face it; we call our best girlfriend from the store to tell her when we stumble on a great sale. How much more should we want to tell her about the deal of the century—that we can trade our sin-stained rags for free, eternally white robes of righteousness!

Sadly, that zeal often fades over time. Maybe because we're slowly surrounded by believers and have little contact with the "Samaritans" of the world. Or maybe because wearing that robe of white somehow becomes a bit routine. Or perhaps we just let our spiritual eyesight dim as we focus intently on everyday life.

I wonder if there ever came a point when this woman's zeal faded. After leading her friends and family to Jesus, did she settle in to live a life of faith without evangelism? Did she simply savor the living water in the years to come, or did she continue to share this living water with others who scarcely knew how thirsty they were until they met her?

How long lasting was her memory of that day at the well? Did it fuel her desire to talk about Jesus for decades to come?

Forget-Me-Nots

I have found it vital to simply *remember.*

How can we tell others who God is and what He has done, in history or in our own lives, if we forget ourselves? They want and need specifics. They've heard that "God is great, and God is good." They want evidence—stories from our own lives that show it.

In our generation it is not enough to argue that Jesus is real and that His kingdom is at hand. People today want to know that His way truly works. Our sister from Samaria ran back to town insisting, "This man told me everything I ever did!" I'm sure she gave examples. Her testimony intrigued people enough to check Jesus out for themselves. Can you recall God-stories from your life that could inspire others to check Jesus out for themselves? Yahweh Sisters, we need to record and remember these stories.

I possessed a superb memory in the BC era (that is, *before* birthing *children*). Now I can't remember recipes I make multiple times a year. I have to look them up each time. I forget appointments if they're not inputted in my Outlook calendar *and* set to email me a reminder. If I enter the market without a list, I inevitably forget an item or two.

Forgetting unless it's written down is a common symptom of our modern lives. We live in a literate culture, where we rely on the ability to look up information as needed. Ancient culture was different. The ancients transmitted information orally. Out of necessity, remembering and reciting received emphasis.

Let me ask, how do you treat the Bible? As a source of reference to use when needed or as a source of life and wisdom to memorize, internalize, and recite? The answer to that question is telling. It's not only indicative of the culture in which we live, but it's a barometer of our personal spirituality.

Today I shopped with a list, yet still forgot something. Sad, I know. So, how will I remember what the Bible teaches if I don't read it regularly to remind myself? What if I don't write down any of it, memorize it, or recite it?

Being a word girl, I'm highly motivated by what I read. For instance, when I read a magazine article about "Six Ways to Get Quality Sleep," I can hardly wait to put it into practice that evening. But weeks or months later, I forget the article and the importance of arranging my life to rest well, and I slide into sloppy sleep patterns.

So I created a "remember this" notebook, filling a binder with inspiring articles and quotes, handwritten notes, verses, and vibrant pictures that motivate me to arrange my life in accordance with my beliefs. Flipping through it a few times a month keeps me focused; I remember, and therefore do, what is important to me.

Why would I need anything less to stay on track spiritually? I have similar sources of remembrance detailing my spiritual beliefs and experiences. I keep record of what God does in and through me so I can remind myself, thank Him, and tell both loved ones and acquaintances of His power.

Do you keep any record of how God has answered your prayers or given you the desires of your heart? Can you recite details of His endless faithfulness at a moment's notice? I journal these things so I will remember. And I rely on those journals for needed motivation when life gets tough.

Journaling is a powerful way to absorb what God is teaching us and to later recall what we've learned. It provides space to chronicle, question, process, probe, or note new insights. It's tempting to assume we'll remember today's blessing or the inspired thought that amazed us, but then life happens, the details grow fuzzy and are forgotten with time.

Women keep track of so many things: committee meetings, appliance manuals, shopping lists, tax records, birth certificates, and bank statements. Plus we're tracking birthdays, anniversaries, and holidays so we can send cute cards. Doesn't it make sense that we need help remembering the truly important stuff—the secret, sacred stuff?

Besides, if God writes things down for future reference, shouldn't we?

The word *remember* appears nearly 150 times in the King James Bible, and nearly 170 times in the NIV—many more if variations of the word are included. In the Old Testament, God frequently instructed His people to build stone memorials to remember how He delivered them. In the New Testament, Jesus models communion and tells us to do this in *remembrance* of Him and His sacrifice. I believe today's Yahweh Sisters should strive to remember what God has done for us. Let's put "record and remember" on our action list and start today.

Ready and Willing

As a young Christian working in a bar all those years ago, I prayed for opportunities to tell people around me about Jesus in kind but convincing ways. I still pray for that.

What about you—do you pray for opportunities to share your faith? Are you prepared to seize them when they arise? Sweet Sisters, let's *carpe diem* and share our stories of faith! It's never as hard as we think.

Oh sure, we might be a little inconvenienced now and then. For instance, I may have to break from my agenda to pick up on God's and share His secrets with someone He's put in my path. Or I might have to stay late somewhere, comfort someone who is hurting, talk to someone who looks different from me, or even drive to the wrong side of town at 3:00 a.m. Is this too much to ask for the chance to increase the kingdom of God?

Are you speaking His name, thereby recording your own on God's remembrance list? In Colossians 4:2–6 (CEV), Paul encourages us to pray for these opportunities and season our conversations with wisdom and grace:

> Never give up praying. And when you pray, keep alert and be thankful. Be sure to pray that God will make a way for us to spread his message and explain the mystery about Christ, even though I am in jail for doing this.

> Please pray that I will make the message as clear as possible.

> When you are with unbelievers, always make good use of the time. Be pleasant and hold their interest when you speak the message. Choose your words carefully and be ready to give answers to anyone who asks questions.

As Yahweh Sisters, this is our task—the Great Commission given to all God's gals. So how can we record, recall, and recite God's wondrous works? Any number of ways: blogging, tweeting, scrapbooking, volunteering, Facebooking, teaching, serving on mission trips, or just meeting others over a cup of hot coffee and engaging in beyond-surface-level chat.

My online friend Melanie recently wrote, "I am aware of blessings that God gives me but I have not kept good records to share with my children or grandchildren. I am considering keeping record in photos." Melanie then wrote a blog post about several ways God recently blessed her and included a photo with each story.

My friend Zoe keeps a "blessings bucket," a simple tin bucket saved from a time her husband surprised her with flowers. After the flowers wilted, she used the bucket to stash notes, cards, verses, and keepsakes that remind her of the many ways God takes care of her.

Another sweet gal, Linny, keeps a "memento box" where she saves all kinds of things—a plastic baggie, a Lego shark, a rock, a broken watch. Each piece symbolically tells the story of a specific time God proved Himself faithful in her life. And on Mondays, she posts the stories on her blog. Reading them builds my faith.

These girls are all God's recording artists, making the effort to record and proclaim His power and provision. I'm certain their names will reach God's scroll.

Treasure, Bling, and Remembered Things

In the book of Malachi, in the same spot where we discovered Yahweh records the names of those who speak of Him, we see that He has a great purpose for His people: to turn rebellious sinners into jewels, God's treasured possessions.

He receives us as we are, washes us in Christ's blood, fills us with living water, places a secret-decoder ring on our finger, promises us a future marriage to His own Son, and begins fashioning us into divine bling. Why? Because He loves us and created us to reflect His beautiful image.

Read the passage in Malachi from *The Message*:

> Then those whose lives honored God got together and talked it over. God saw what they were doing and listened in. A book was opened in God's presence and minutes were taken of the meeting, with the names of the God-fearers written down, all the names of those who honored God's name.
>
> God-of-the-Angel-Armies said, "They're mine, all mine. They'll get special treatment when I go into action. I treat them with the same consideration and kindness that parents give the child who honors them. Once more you'll see the difference it makes between being a person who does the right thing and one who doesn't, between serving God and not serving him." (Mal. 3:16–25 MSG)

Pause to feel the pleasured pride with which God declares, "You are mine, all mine!" Verse 17 in the New King James reads this way: "'They shall be Mine,' says the LORD of hosts, 'On the day that I make them My jewels …'" The notion that I am a gem in God's sight warms me to my bling-lovin' core.

I know we want our loved ones and neighbors to belong to Him. I know we want them to discover the difference serving God makes.

I know you want to be His secret-keeper and His secret-revealer. And I know you can. Deuteronomy 29:29 (ESV) says, "The secret things belong to the LORD our God, but the things that are revealed belong to us and to our children forever, that we may do all the words of this law."

So, my treasured Yahweh Sister, will you be God's secret-keeper and His secret-revealer? Record your answer, and remember your zeal. And know that I'm right here beside you. We'll be recording, remembering, revealing, and reciting these secrets of the kingdom of God together.

I hope your name is next to mine on the list!

BIBLE STUDY

1. My heart longs to know and keep God's secrets. I also long to share them. That's why I wrote this book. I consider it the greatest gift I can offer—not because my writing is stellar, but because God's Word is out-of-this-world true. Read Matthew 13:52. How does Jesus describe Sisters who share His secrets with others? What does Christ liken them to?

2. Paul said we should be thought of "as servants of Christ and as those entrusted with the secret things of God" (1 Cor. 4:1 NIV). He added that "those who have been given a trust must prove faithful" (v. 2 NIV). Are you faithfully sharing the Sisterhood secrets? What holds you back?

3. The early chapters of the book of Joshua detail the Israelites, under Joshua's leadership and with the help of God, seizing the land God promised them. At one point they needed to cross an overflowing Jordan River. God parted the river for them. Read the story in Joshua 3 and 4. What did Joshua and the people do following this miracle (Josh. 4:19–24)? Why?

4. Look up these verses. Note what each one teaches you about remembering.

Exodus 20:8

Exodus 20:23

Numbers 15:39

Deuteronomy 5:15

Deuteronomy 8:18

Psalm 111:3–5

Luke 22:19

Acts 20:30–32

1 Thessalonians 4:1–2

1 Timothy 5:24–25

2 Timothy 1:3–7

Hebrews 10:34–36

1 Peter 1:16–18

1 Peter 5:9

2 Peter 3:1–3

5. Read 1 Peter 3:15. Write an answer to the question, "Why should you harbor hope?"

Epilogue

If you can't already tell, there are several things I cherish deeply in life—such as inspiring words, my secret decoder ring, and my Sisters in Christ. It took all three to get me through the writing of this book.

In the final weeks before my manuscript was due, my mother-in-law was diagnosed with stage-four lung cancer. She underwent radiation but chose to refuse chemotherapy, setting her on a course for rapid descent. I had to tell my children that evening their grandmother was dying.

When the diagnosis came, three chapters remained in various stages of completion: "Get By with a Little Help from Your Friends," "Turn the Beat Around," and "Don't Be Afraid in the Dark." Turns out, they were all topics I would experience in a fresh way as I lived them and typed them.

One week before my manuscript was due, I posted a plea for prayer on my blog. Multiple comments and emails came in every day, right up until the final hour of my deadline. Those words encouraged me. Thank you, sweet cyber friends.

I also emailed my teammates at Proverbs 31 Ministries, asking them to pray for my family and my ability to concentrate and finish these chapters. They prayed—I felt it.

Then my friend Lysa suggested I email the team any chapters I was stuck on and ask for their help. Smiling at the irony, I sent them "Get By with a Little Help from Your Friends," which was only 80 percent done. So if that was your favorite chapter, you partly have them to thank. Special appreciation to Lysa, Holly, Melanie, and Glynnis for their help.

The Sunday before my deadline, I made what felt a risky choice to walk away from my last unfinished chapter and rest my weary soul. I had to "turn my beat around." My whole family was dragging under the weight of grief and stress that morning. We needed to reconnect with God and one another, to refuel our emotional and spiritual battery packs. That's just what we did over church, a good meal, and some precious family snuggle time.

Come Monday, "D-day," I finished "Don't Be Afraid in the Dark." As I wrote I got the distinct sense that I'd be calling upon every point and verse in that chapter in the days ahead. Girls, the winds are blowing in my family right now as we face the impending loss of a loved one, but I am looking to Jesus. I'm insisting, "Lord, call me to You on the water" as I sling one leg over the boat's edge to head toward Him.

I say all this to acknowledge life is hard. It can be tiring and unpredictable. People and relationships can inconvenience you or complicate things you thought you had all smoothed out. But the God-sized secrets revealed in this book are true and trustworthy. You can count on them, your Yahweh Sisters, and Jesus to pull you through. And I pray that you always will.

Sweet Blessings,
Rachel

P.S. Feel free to stop by my blog at www.RachelOlsen.com and introduce yourself—I love meeting new Yahweh Sisters! I'd also love to hear how this book impacted you.

Notes

Chapter 2: Know When to Pay Retail

1. Matthew Henry, *Commentary on the Whole Bible* (Peabody, MA: Hendrickson Publishers, 2008), 1336.

2. Ibid.

Chapter 3: Kill Your Competition

1. C. S. Lewis, *Mere Christianity* (New York: HarperCollins, 2001), 126.

2. Ibid., 122.

3. C. J. Mahaney, *Humility: True Greatness* (Colorado Springs: Multnomah, 2005), 22.

4. Paul J. Achtemeier, ed., *The HarperCollins Bible Dictionary* (San Francisco: HarperCollins, 1996), s.v "humility."

5. Lewis, *Mere Christianity*, 127.

6. Ibid., 128.

7. C. S. Lewis, *The Weight of Glory* (New York: HarperCollins, 2001), 37–38.

Chapter 5: Have Eyes Bigger Than Your Stomach

1. Lewis, *Mere Christianity*, 120.

2. Randy Alcorn, *Money, Possessions, and Eternity* (Carol Stream, IL: Tyndale House, 2003), 98.

Chapter 6: Don't Be Afraid in the Dark

1. Walker Percy, *The Moviegoer* (New York: Vintage Books, 1960), 13.

2. John Ortberg, *If You Want to Walk on Water, You've Got to Get Out of the Boat* (Grand Rapids, MI: Zondervan, 2001), 78.

Chapter 7: Adjust Your Scale

1. Merriam-Webster Online, s.v. "perfect," www.merriam-webster.com/dictionary/perfect (accessed June 14, 2010).

2. Matthew Henry, *Commentary on the Whole Bible,* 1706, www.biblestudytools.com/commentaries/matthew-henry-complete (accessed March 2, 2009).

Chapter 8: Get By With a Little Help from Your Friends

1. Gary Smalley, *The DNA of Relationships* (Carol Stream, IL:Tyndale House, 2004), 124.

Chapter 9: Turn the Beat Around

1. Mark Buchanan, *The Rest of God* (Nashville: Thomas Nelson, 2006), 45.

2. Eugene Peterson, *Living the Message: Daily Help for Living the God-Centered Life* (San Francisco: HarperCollins, 1996), 90.

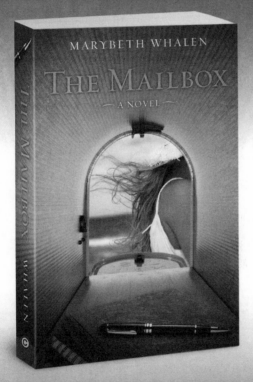

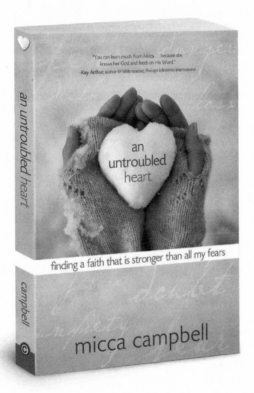

"Rachel Olsen has created the ultimate godly girlfriends' guide—completely contemporary yet biblically solid; poignant yet practical. Her clever, warm, and vulnerable style imparts a fresh and needed dose of perspective to all of God's girls."

Karen Ehman, national speaker for Proverbs 31 Ministries and author of *A Life That Says Welcome* and *The Complete Guide to Getting and Staying Organized*

ARE YOU TIRED OF LIFE AS USUAL?

Done with feeling exhausted—or worse, bored? Ready to trade your issues and hang-ups for greater intimacy and fulfillment? Then it's time you did some digging for biblical "bling" and discovered the shining secrets to life in God's kingdom. Rachel's writing is lighthearted and fun, but she's serious about helping you uncover biblical secrets that can make your life shine. This book will help you:

- ♥ Overcome the comparisons and competitive urges that leave you lonely
- ♥ Accept help from others
- ♥ Discover God's surprising source of spiritual beauty and strength
- ♥ Embrace your need for rest
- ♥ Find adventure as you yield wholeheartedly to God
- ♥ Dig into the Bible for yourself and understand what you find there

Grab your Bible and a girlfriend, and come discover twelve secrets the world doesn't know.

Photo by Tom Sapp

RACHEL OLSEN is a popular national women's speaker, a staffer with Proverbs 31 Ministries, and a communication instructor at the University of North Carolina, Wilmington. She served as a writer and general editor for *God's Purpose for Every Woman*. Rachel and her family enjoy life in a beach town in the Carolinas.

David C Cook®
transforming lives together
www.davidccook.com